Also by Edlin D. Rochford

COMMUNICATION STUDIES:
Preparing Students For CAPE
[Revised Edition]

CAPE COMMUNICATION STUDIES:

Practical Exercises for Paper 02 Essays

EDLIN D. ROCHFORD

CAPE COMMUNICATION STUDIES:
PRACTICAL EXERCISES FOR PAPER 02 ESSAYS

iUniverse books may be ordered through booksellers or by contacting:

iUniverse
1663 Liberty Drive
Bloomington, IN 47403
www.iuniverse.com
1-800-Authors (1-800-288-4677)

Because of the dynamic nature of the Internet, any web addresses or links contained in this book may have changed since publication and may no longer be valid. The views expressed in this work are solely those of the author and do not necessarily reflect the views of the publisher, and the publisher hereby disclaims any responsibility for them.

Any people depicted in stock imagery provided by Thinkstock are models,
and such images are being used for illustrative purposes only.
Certain stock imagery © Thinkstock.

ISBN: 978-1-4917-7590-5 (sc)
ISBN: 978-1-4917-7589-9 (e)

Print information available on the last page.

iUniverse rev. date: 10/29/2015

Dedication

I have been overly blessed by the thousands of students and by extension their families who have crossed my path as a teacher. CAPE Communication Studies: A Practical Guide to Paper O2 Essays is the outcome of my continued effort to ensure that all students are guaranteed the highest grade in this subject.

Acknowledgements

All illustrations are the created property of PRESENTERMEDIA
Ms. Sharlee Barkarr for choosing and placing all PRESENTERMEDIA illustrations
Photography by Ms. Allison Punch of Fotocraft Ltd
Editing and reviewing by Mr. Philip G. Rochford HBM

Contents

SECTION C - MODULE THREE ESSAYS 81

Introduction

My professional worth is intricately connected with my students' academic achievement-
Edlin Dianne Joseph Rochford

Ever since I published in 2008 my first book *Communication Studies: Preparing Students for CAPE*, I have been bombarded with requests from both students and teachers throughout the Caribbean to address the requirements of the essay component in Paper 02 of the examination; writing this book is my attempt to fulfil their requests.

CAPE Communication Studies: A Practical Guide to Paper 02 Essays is structured in such a way that users are given the opportunity to review each of the three modules. The various essay questions are closely aligned to the requirements of the Communication Studies Syllabus so that for the students, perfect practice will provide perfect examination delivery! A template that can be customized to suit the specific requirements of each essay is provided.

Fun activities that test their knowledge of the content of each module are also included. For example in Module One, students will be able to assess how well they can distinguish the reliability and validity of information. Additionally, in Module Two, there are group activities which develop their understanding of language and community. Finally, activities in Module Three test whether the students understand the dynamics involved in the entire communication process. This testing ultimately enables the student to fill the missing information so identified.

CAPE was introduced in Trinidad and Tobago in 2004, and from its inception I began teaching Communication Studies; Two years later I became an assistant examiner for the subject in the annual marking exercise and for the last 3 years I have been a table leader. The results of my students reveal that of the total number my record of success in CAPE from 2004 to present will show that of the total 425 student s that I've sent up for the exam 94.1% got ones, 1.2% got twos and 4.7% got threes.

SECTION A

1. THE FORMAT OF MODULE ONE ESSAY QUESTION IN PAPER 02

In the Module 1 essay students are asked to read an extract and respond to the instructions. The instructions will be similar to the following:

a. State the speaker or writer's main point.
b. Write an essay of approximately 500 words in which you include reference to the following:
   (i) The speaker's DOMINANT purpose
   (ii) Identify the (**specific pieces of information**) organizational strategies and language techniques that the writer or speaker or poet used to help him or her to achieve that purpose.
   (iii) Comment on the reliability and validity of the information. (**optional**)
   (iv) Evaluate the validity of the information presented. (**optional**)
   (v) Comment on the appropriateness of tone and register. (**optional**)

[**25 marks**]

2. MARKING SCHEME WITH ALLOCATION OF MARKS FOR MODULE 1 ESSAY

Content – **10 marks**

(a)   The Main Idea

Award **2 marks** for an answer that fully captures the expected answer.
Award **1 mark** for an answer that partially captures the expected answer.

(b)   Purpose

Award **2 marks** for an answer that fully captures content and purpose.
Award **1 mark** for partial content connected to an appropriate purpose verb.
Do not award any marks for an appropriate purpose verb only.

(c)   Language techniques used

Award **2 marks** for mention and explanation of **TWO** techniques.
Award **1 mark** for mention of any **TWO** techniques without explanation
OR Award **1 mark** for mention of **TWO** techniques but with an explanation of one

(d)   Organisational strategies

Award **1 mark** for mention of **EACH** strategy

(e)   Appropriateness of tone   **(Optional)**

Award **1 mark** for mention of an appropriate tone
Award **1 mark** for discussion

Organisation	7
Excellent introduction, thematic cohesion in paragraphs, appropriate use of transitional devices, effective conclusion.	7
Good use of the above with one to two weaknesses.	**5-6**
Adequate level of organisation with several weaknesses noted.	**3-4**

Unsatisfactory level of organisation. Weaknesses in all areas identified above.	1-2

Expression	8
Excellent, effective and error-free use of language.	8
Very good use of language though there may be a few lapses.	7
Good use of language though there may be a few lapses.	5-6
Some ability to use language accurately and effectively, but with some inconsistency in accurate usage.	3-4
Frequent, inaccurate use of language. **OR** Insufficient information presented.	1-2
Inability to use language accurately. **OR** Too little information presented to make an assessment.	0

3.   IDENTIFYING THE WRITER'S MAIN POINT

- The **main idea** is the **most general** and **important statement** that the writer makes about the topic
- The main idea is what the writer is **writing about**, the **idea that you as reader get as you read or is left with after you are finished reading.**
- The main idea is **always definitive and balanced!** Sometimes students make the mistake and write only the **negatives and omit the positives of the topic.**
- If you were asked the questions, **"What is the piece about?"** and **"What is the writer saying about it?"** your responses will be what you determine is the main idea.
- The main idea **is never a verb** so it can never be stated like this 'The main idea of this passage is **to inform**...'
- An example of how to state the main idea can be, 'The main idea of the piece **is that** students have problems answering the Module One essay...".

4. IDENTIFYING THE WRITER'S PURPOSE

- To **understand or know why** the writer wrote the piece is to understand the writer's purpose.
- To analyse that is to examine **what was written and how it was written** is to understand the writer's purpose.
- It is what the writer **wants to happen as a result of your reading the piece**.
- The writer's purpose/intent **is always** stated as **a verb**!
- Being aware of the writer's purpose when you read helps you evaluate how well the writer has achieved the purpose and decide whether he or she has convinced you as a reader.
- The active reader reads more than the words and more than even the ideas: *the active reader reads what the writer is doing.*
- The active reader **reconstructs both the strategies and the techniques** that the writer used to realize the purpose.
- Likewise the writer's **overall or dominant purpose determines the techniques** he or she uses.

  ➢ For example, a purpose for the list of stock market prices in the daily newspaper can be "to report information needed for making new decisions."
  ➢ An editorial in the same paper might be considered specifically "to criticize the actions" of a particular public official.
  ➢ The purpose of the comic strips would be "to entertain"
  ➢ The use of personal anecdotes in any given piece might suggest that the writer is seeking your emotional response or sympathetic involvement in the material
  ➢ The heavy use of statistics in an excerpt suggests that the writer's major purpose is to provide documentation and proof of the particular topic.
  ➢ The writer's purpose might be to persuade the reader of the attraction of the island as a nature lover's paradise.
  ➢ The writer's purpose is to criticise the behaviour of the government's policy on crime.

5. IDENTIFYING THE LANGUAGE TECHNIQUES AND ORGANIZATIONAL STRATEGIES

When you are asked to identify both the **language techniques** and the **organizational strategies** that the writer used to help achieve the dominant purpose of the piece, what you are really being asked to do is to identify the pieces of information (found in the techniques and strategies) that the writer carefully and specifically used to get the message across.

6. EXAMPLES OF SOME LANGUAGE TECHNIQUES FOUND IN MODULE ONE ESSAY

All **Similes** use '**like**' or '**as**' in comparison, and are effective in helping the writer achieve two purposes; firstly similes give the reader a truly vivid picture of the situation for clarity and secondly it always evokes some sort of response in the reader.

Many times similes and metaphors are also used as forms of imagery.

Personification gives inanimate or non-living things only human qualities and not just any qualities. Some students make the mistake by not asking if the quality is a human quality: if you ask that question and the answer is 'no' then it is not a personification. This device is effective in that, by imbuing the object with human qualities, the writer is emphasising connection and piquing the reader's interest in the theme.

The purpose of imagery in literary works is to generate a vibrant and graphic presentation of a scene that appeals to as many of the reader's senses as possible.

Visual Imagery

Visual imagery is as simple as it sounds: It describes something you can see. Visual imagery will describe a setting's colours, size, shape, physical features and anything else that you detect with your eyes. Visual imagery creates the vivid mental picture you see as you read.

Auditory Imagery

Auditory imagery, also known as aural imagery, describes something you can hear. It can be used on a large scale, such as describing the sounds of an earthquake, or it can be more subtle, such as the sound of an individual's footsteps on a wooden floor.

Tactile Imagery

Tactile imagery appeals to your sense of touch. It describes parts of the story you can feel. Good tactile imagery should make you feel something as though it were really there.

Olfactory Imagery

Olfactory imagery describes something you can smell. Writers can use lots of creative license with olfactory imagery by assigning smells to unusual things. For example a writer can use olfactory imagery to describe the smell of a forest after it rains or the strong smell of a fresh cup of herb tea.

Gustatory Imagery

Gustatory imagery describes something you can taste. Like olfactory imagery, gustatory imagery has endless possibilities for describing simple things in a creative way. Gustatory imagery can describe anything from the taste of a slice of pizza to the taste in your mouth before you have to make a big speech.

Kinaesthetic Imagery

It is a broad term that is used to describe various emotions. It includes sense of touch, movement, feeling and temperature, internal emotions and physical interactions.

Examples of other language techniques are **rhetorical question, alliteration, anecdote, repetition, contrast, comparison, long complex sentences, complex phrasing, use of quotation marks to highlight a specific point, and the use of 'we' to include the reader.**

7. EXAMPLES OF ORGANIZATIONAL STRATEGIES FOUND IN MODULE ONE ESSAY

Historical data such as photographs, artefacts, documents from court hearings, newspapers and documentaries are effective in that they all add in some way to the reliability and credibility of the extract.

Use of short paragraphs to put forward an argument is effective in that in most cases the information comes across in a simple manner.

Presentation of a chronological outline of the development of events

Presentation of an overview: this strategy gives the reader a general idea of the theme and is effective in that it helps to make the main idea and purpose clearer.

Opinion of a reliable source: this is effective in that the readers like to know that well known persons have a say in the matter. This adds to the credibility and reliability of the information.

8. EFFECTIVENESS OF ORGANIZATIONAL STRATEGIES AND LANGUAGE TECHNIQUES

When you have identified a technique you need to specify what it is (do not give line number alone) and then you must write about **the effectiveness of the device.**

When you write about effectiveness you are writing about:

- what the device is adding to the piece
- how the device is impacting on your senses
- how the device is adding to your understanding of the piece
- and most importantly how the device is helping to achieve the writer's purpose

Following these two simple steps will help you to write about the effectiveness of each organizational strategy and language technique:-

1. Remember or look back at the Verb that you used in the purpose.

2. Ask this question, **"How is this Personification helping to** persuade **the reader to visit St John?"** or this question, **"How is referencing an expert helping to** persuade **nature lovers to visit St John?"**

For many students the challenge is **not to define** the devices but rather to **identify appropriate** examples (use quotation marks) from the passage to support and then say how they add or why you believe that the writer used them and how in rare cases they took away from the piece.

As with every essay one must have **proper organisation**. There must be an opening, a body for the content and a conclusion where no new ideas must be introduced. The correct use of **transitional** words will enhance your essay. Refrain from making your essay read like a list of devices. For example do not say the first, the second and so on.

Critical reasoning to the rescue: In an exam and you are stuck, try doing critical reasoning by looking at the writer's style. For example, when someone gives a speech, she uses intonation (voice pitch, volume, speed) and gestures and inflections to get her point across, or to make her intentions clear. A writer, however, relies on writing style to do the same thing. Pay attention to the way words are written and sentences structured because they can give some insight into the writer's intention.

Tone is the attitude of the author towards the topic that he or she is writing about. **Tone** is closely linked to the writer's purpose. One easy way of understanding tone is to ask *"what attitude did I get from reading the author's words?"*

Always use Adjectives such as **persuasive, sarcastic, formal, informative, humorous, mysterious, critical and straight-forward** to describe the writer's tone.

Finally, the best way to overcome this challenge in Module One essay is to practice writing this type of essay!

9. DETERMINING THE CREDIBILITY OF SOURCES

As students you will have to determine if the information you are getting is from a valid, reliable source. For example, if you were interested in researching the effects of tobacco on disease or addiction, would a tobacco company site be an appropriate sole location from which to get all information?

Because data is used in selective ways to express information, it generally represents a point of view of the presenter. Every writer wants to prove his or her point, and will use the data and information that assists in doing so.

When evaluating information from the various sources that's available, it is important to examine who is providing the "*information*", and what might be their point of view or bias.

For example the popularity of the Internet makes it the perfect medium for commercial and socio-political publishing.

10. STUDENTS' ACTIVITY #1: **HOW MUCH DO YOU KNOW ABOUT VALIDITY AND RELIABILITY OF INFORMATION?**

Below are criteria you can use to evaluate the **validity and reliability** of information that you may obtain from various sources. Match the questions to a possible answer.

#	Questions to ask	Possible answer
1.	Are all aspects of the subject covered? Is only one point of view presented?	
2.	Is the information in the resource accurate? Are there political or ideological biases? What motivation does the author have for placing this information on the internet?	
3.	Is the information covered fact, opinion, or propaganda? Does the information appear to be valid and well-researched, or is it questionable and unsupported by evidence? Assumptions should be reasonable. Note errors or omissions. Is the author's point of view objective and impartial? Is the language free of emotion-rousing words and bias?	
4.	Is the information factual, or opinion? Does the site contain original information, or simply links?	
5.	Is the text well written? Is there a conclusion, theme? Are there spelling and grammatical errors?	
6.	How frequently is the resource updated, is it a static resource? Are dates of update stated, and do these correspond to the information in the resource? Does the organization or person hosting the resource appear to have a commitment to ongoing maintenance and stability of the resource?	
7.	What is the purpose of the resource? Is this clearly stated? Does the resource fulfil the stated purpose?	

8.	Who are the intended users of this resource? At what level is the resource pitched: a subject expert, a layperson, or a school student? Will the resource satisfy the needs of the intended users?	
9.	To what level of detail in the subject does the resource go? How much information is given? How broad is the topic area? How in-depth is the information?	
10.	Does the resource have some reputable organization or expert behind it? Does the author have standing in the field? Are sources of information stated? Is the information verifiable? Can the author be contacted for clarification or to be informed of new information?	

List of possible answers

• Content	• Quality of writing
• Audience	• Accuracy
• Depth or scope	• Purpose
• Breadth	• Currency
• Objective Reasoning	• Authority

11. STUDENTS' ACTIVITY #2: ORGANIZATIONAL STRATEGIES AND LANGUAGE TECHNIQUES

How well can you identify some of the organizational strategies (OS) and the language techniques (LT) found in Module 1 extracts?

#	Examples	OS	LT
1.	Use of the acronym UNESCO that is a reputable international organization in the extract		
2.	Presentation of a number of ways in which the topic is explained		
3.	Contrast of the effects of the theme of illiteracy		
4.	Repetition		
5.	The use of academic language		

6.	Use of humour		
7.	Use of contractions in the dialogue of the extract		
8.	Use of short sentences or paragraphs		
9.	Use of analogy		
10.	Definition of the term		
11.	Conversational tone or style		
12.	Presentation of details in a sequential timeline		
13.	Use of rhetorical questions		
14.	Use of specialist or expert opinion		
15.	Use of steps –in- a- process approach		
16.	Use of comparison and contrast		
17.	Use of factual data from studies done		
18.	Use of literary devices		
19.	Use of 2nd person pronouns to directly address the reader		

12. SUGGESTIONS FOR WRITING YOUR BEST MODULE ONE ESSAYS
Using the **"PEE"** format for Module One essay where **P** stands for **Point**, **E** stands for **Example** and **E** stands for **Explanation**.

You can modify this format to satisfy the requirements of all 3 essays of Paper 02. In Module One essay here is how you use the **PEE** format:-

After responding to the Main Point, the Purpose and the fact that the writer used language techniques and organizational strategies to help achieve purpose you are to then write the paragraphs.

Firstly in each paragraph you utilise the **P-** by making a **Point** to identify either the organizational strategy or language technique which you are going to discuss.

Secondly you utilize the **E-**by giving a supporting **Example** taken from the excerpt. Do not write line number but write out the words. You may use Ellipsis, **only** if you know how to use it correctly, otherwise as I have cautioned my students, for safety sake, please write out the entire example of the strategy or technique.

Thirdly you write about the second **E**-by giving an **Explanation** to the question, '**How does this example of the strategy or technique help the writer to achieve the purpose?**' Your explanation is also about whether the said strategy or technique was used effectively in the excerpt to achieve the intended purpose.

NB: You do this for **all** the organizational strategies and language techniques that they asked you to discuss!

13.   MODULE 1 - ESSAY QUESTIONS FOR PRACTICE

SECTION A
MODULE 1 – GATHERING and PROCESSING INFORMATION

Read the excerpt below carefully and answer the questions that follow

The term rape culture was first coined in the 1970s second wave feminists, during a time when efforts had been made to increase awareness about the prevalence of rape because previously, most Americans assumed that rape, incest and wife-beating rarely happened. Sociology professor Joyce E. Williams traced the origin of the first usage of the term rape culture to the 1975 documentary film *Rape Culture* produced and directed by Margaret Lazarus and Renner Wunderlich for Cambridge Documentary films.

So what are the causes of sexual violence? Nicholas Groth, Ph.D. a clinical psychologist developed a well-known and well-researched typology for adult male sex offenders that was developed in 1979 and is detailed in his book *Men Who Rape: The Psychology of the Offender*. The many types of rapes include rape motivated by angst, power, and sadism and gang culture for sexual gratification. Though anger and power are believed, by some academics, to be the primary motivation for most rapes, in 1994, Richard Falcourt a professor of Crime, Law, and Justice and Sociology at Pennsylvania State University and Madga Moots, an adjunct professor of Psychology of Down State University at Albany, co-authored the book The Anatomy of Rape: The Socialists Viewpoint which argues that sexual fulfilment and gratification are the driving force of rapists, rather than the aggressive desire to dominate the victim. The authors believed that rape is an aggressive form of deep sexual coercion and the ultimate goal of the act of rape is immediate sexual satisfaction rather that the sexual power that so many researchers purported.

Well, is there a link between our local and regional music and rape culture? The objectification of women is commonly associated with rape culture and unfortunately, this is often seen in the lyrics of songs and the music videos associated with them. The music that is produce both locally and regionally is mainly soca and dancehall. Although there are other genres, these two are the most common and mainstream forms of music in our society especially among young people. Trinidadian, Shal Marshall, a popular radio personality released a song for the 2015 carnival season entitled, *Motivation*. The lyrics of the song generally did not promote a sexual objectification of women but sadly the same cannot be said for the music video. Right from the start there were women dressed in very revealing underwear and were basically there to just gyrate their bodies. With Carnival being a very integral part of our Caribbean culture, sexuality is amped up when promoting anything pertaining to carnival due to the nature of the celebrations with wining and increased alcohol consumption, but when does it get to the point where we have to ask, is this going too far?

What can we do to prevent us as a country from becoming a rape culture? In Trinidad and Tobago, as of January the 20th, 2013, according to data from the Police Service's Crime and Problem Analysis branch (CAPA), 3956 sexual offences were reported between January 1st, 2008 and December 30, 2012. These statistics are even more distressing when one realises that the majority of rapes and other sexual assaults are never reported. According to researchers in the University of Surrey in the UK, these alarming statistics can be due to the commonly held attitudes towards rape. Fearing that they would not be believed and not wanting to get their attacker in trouble.

As a nation there needs to be a more solidly, serious approach to treating with the problem of rape and some ways that we can prevent our country from becoming a rape culture are a greater encouragement of reporting the crime, training teachers with up to date methods on identifying signs of abuse in their students and more discussions as to how we as men and women of this country want its citizens to be valued. Should human beings be valued for their bodies, their minds or their souls?

Write an ESSAY, in no more than 500 words, in which you:

a. State the writer's main point
b. State the **DOMINANT** purpose of the passage.
c. Discuss the effectiveness of **THREE** organizational strategies and **THREE** language techniques used by the writer used to achieve that purpose.
d. Evaluate the validity of the information presented.

Total 25 marks

SECTION A
MODULE 1 – GATHERING and PROCESSING INFORMATION

Read the excerpt below and answer the questions that follow.

According to *Dictionary.com*, music can be defined as, "An art of sound in time that expresses ideas and emotions in significant forms through the elements of rhythm, melody, harmony and colour." Plato the philosopher defined music as, "A moral law that gives soul to the universe, wings to the mind, flight to the imagination and charm and gaiety to life and to everything." The different genres such as Soca, Rock, Gospel, Reggae and Rap all have varying effects on the listener.

For teens struggling to find their own selfhood, music provides them an outlet for personal identity, development and expression.

The music teenagers listen to is often said to have an effect on their actions. Certain genres of music, such as rap and heavy metal, have been targeted and blamed for delinquent teen behaviours.

According to a 2009 American Academy of Paediatrics study entitled, "Impact of Music, Music Lyrics and Music Videos on Children and Youth," music messages that expose teens to violent, explicit, and or sexual themes and stereotypes or to substance abuse can potentially produce significant changes in their mood or behaviour.

This point was also supported by a study done by Brad Reddick at Harvard Medical School.

Even regional genres such as Dancehall and Soca have been linked to negative behaviour exhibited by teens, and research showed that this was mainly due to their lyrical content. Research indicated that, in Jamaica for example, Dancehall music has come under fire because of the lyrics and images it creates as it depicts violence, high sexual behaviours or misbehaviours and erosion of moral fibre.

Eighty percent (80%) of the teenagers interviewed stated that music in one way or the other has affected their behaviour. Many of them indicated that the lyrics in music can be influential on their behaviour, as they are often inclined to do what the lyrics says to do. If the lyrics are negative they will be inclined to do something negative and vice versa.

One teenager stated that music may influence behaviour, however, the way you behave is ultimately your choice, and therefore music should not be blamed for the actions of teens. We must however acknowledge the role of music in teenage behaviour, and musicians should be made aware of their responsibility in the way their music impacts teenage behaviour.

An article by the Association for Natural Psychology stated that music can be a positive force for mental health, relaxing and intellectual stimulation. The article indicated that music can and does affect our emotions and can create channels in our mind and patterns of thinking. This therefore proves that music can impact teenagers psychologically.

From those interviewed, many of the teens indicated that if they listen to a particular genre regularly, whether it is considered positive or negative music, they find themselves thinking about the song and the lyrics very often. This proves that music can affect your pattern of thinking as stated in the article.

In regional music such as Soca, Dancehall, Reggae, the lyrics are mainly sung in different variation of Creole. Research showed that teenagers who listen to these musical genres speak like the musicians which could be considered a good or bad thing depending on one's perception of Creole. The same may apply for a song which contains Standard English. This again emphasises the critical role of musicians could play in positively impacting the language used by teenagers.

Edlin D. Rochford

a.   State the speaker's main point in approximately 30 words.
b.   Write an ESSAY, in approximately 500 words, in which you include:
  (i)   The speaker's purpose
  (ii)   The effectiveness of at least TWO organizational strategies and TWO language techniques that the speaker used to achieve that purpose.
  (iii) The overall tone of the piece

Total 25 marks

Read the passage below carefully and answer the questions that follow.

Is Vaccination Inhumane?

Do you like being poked and pricked? Do you see being vaccinated as a duty or a right? Many strange theories about vaccines and vaccination are advanced in this present age, and the concrete fact is often neglected. It is needless to argue, in the face of the appalling increase in the death rate that vaccination is a benefit. The following observation is noteworthy:

Three epidemics occurred in the Philippines islands, the first being before 1905, in which it stated that ten percent of the smallpox virus proved fatal. But no systematic vaccination was *ca*rried on at that time. In the first real epidemic of recent years, that which occurred in 1905-6, at which time vaccination was well under way, the death rate was sixteen percent. In 1908-9, when vaccination was more extensively used, the mortality was more than twenty-five percent; daring the recent outbreak of 1918-19 the rate of death was over sixty-five percent.

These figures will bear investigation and can be seen in the report of the Philippine Health Service for 1919 and can be considered an authorized record. Under U. S. Government supervision, the Filipinos have been vaccinated and revaccinated and surely the system has had an opportunity to become very thoroughly tested.

Another example can be seen in 1906 when an improved version of typhoid vaccine was reintroduced for soldiers in India; and inoculation became compulsory for all members of the Indian Civil Service in 1912, though its use among civilians remained limited. During World War I, more than 90% of the volunteer British force in France was immunized, though anti-vaccinationists and liberal politicians ensured that it never became compulsory. By 1911, all American troops were compelled to submit to typhoid inoculation. The pattern becomes clear: biological protection where possible for state officers and military personnel, with intensive hygiene reform of civilians or natives.

Most of the north-eastern states of the United States had compulsory school vaccination laws at this time, though many Midwestern and southern states continued to resist moves to enact vaccination statutes until the 1890s. Not until 1894 did Pennsylvania pass a compulsory school vaccination law, soon after suffering a widespread smallpox outbreak. But by 1900, according to

John Duffy, Pennsylvania had finally established an "effective state-wide program of compulsory vaccination."

Victor G. Heiser, the Director of the Civil Health Service, was particularly proud of the rigor with which he enforced smallpox vaccination in the islands. The annual deaths from smallpox during the Philippine-American war were estimated at 40,000; yet in 1913, only 823 deaths were reported. What, the health authorities asked, was responsible for "this almost unbelievable reduction"? Their answer, quite simply, was vaccination. The chief vaccinator under the Spanish regime had recorded 9,136 vaccinations in Manila between 3 November 1894 and 25 October 1898. In contrast, the American authorities—aware of the "necessity for constant vigilance in this disease"- performed 103,931 vaccinations in 1899 alone, and almost 18 million by 1914. Even so, the coverage of these campaigns was generally more limited than their promoters admitted, with the exception, perhaps, of an unusually thorough general vaccination in 1905. Probably not more than half the vaccinations were successful. Smallpox remained endemic in the archipelago, its incidence increasing again by the 1920s.

Circular No. 147 of the Bureau of Animal Industry and Farmer's Bulletin No. 666 contain proof by the U. S. Government that the epidemics of foot and mouth disease which swept this country in 1902-03, 1908, and 1914 were started from vaccine virus. The same circular No. 147, pages 24-26, states that from 1902 to 1908 and very probably to 1914, thousands of school children were vaccinated under compulsion with virus containing the germs of foot and mouth disease, with a resultant debasement of the blood which may, in after years, result in complications of a very serious nature. It is high time the public awaken to the dangers of vaccine virus, and absolutely refuse to have their bodies violated under so-called health laws.

The major goal of the progressive colonial public health department was the reform of pathological social habits—not, primarily, vaccination, and rarely the improvement of environmental, economic, or industrial conditions.

a. State the writer's main point. **[2 marks]**
b. Write an ESSAY, in approximately 500 words, in which you include:
   (i) The writer's purpose
   (ii) The effectiveness of THREE organizational strategies and THREE language techniques that the writer used to achieve that purpose.

Total 25 marks

SECTION A
MODULE 1 – GATHERING and PROCESSING INFORMATION

Read the excerpt below and answer the questions that follow.

Are you too young to have heard the saying "Home is where the heart is." Or are you one who believes that a house and a home is the same thing . Six o' one haf ah dozen o' de other! Is there a housing crisis in your country? Does your family own the house in which you live? Do you intend to own your own home? Are you worried about not being able to afford your own home in the future?

If you read newspapers you already know that the costs to rent or purchase housing is becoming increasingly less affordable to millions of persons, both for those on fixed retirement incomes as well as those who have not yet reached retirement.

With the "graying of the world" the number of persons 65 years of age and older is growing dramatically and while many in this "age wave" have the financial resources they need, many do not and do not have a clue as to where they will lay their head. This is not only a dilemma but a virtual headache for many on a daily basis. For example Gerald is one of those persons who have only a small pension, and a few assets, his only hope for safe, secure and affordable housing is through units built with the assistance of the government's agency whose mandate it is to create affordable homes for the citizenry. Gerald is just a number on a list that is as long as the time that they told him he has to wait!

In the Caribbean the housing situation continues to be a front burner issue for many governments and stakeholders.

The Barbados-based Caribbean Development Bank (CDB) says it is now revising its "Housing Sector Policy and Strategy" so as to better assist regional countries deal with their housing problems, particularly for low and lower middle-income segments of the population.

The CDB said that recent studies suggest that the housing deficit in Latin America and the Caribbean stands at between 42 and 51 million units in a region that is estimated to grow to 160 million households by 2020.

"Since 1990, CDB has provided over US$160 million in loans and grants to 12 Barbados Mutual Companies in support of various initiatives in the housing sector.

"Traditionally, interventions have been geared towards home ownership, including the provision of mortgage finance through financial intermediaries, improvements in housing stock, upgrading and regularising informal settlements and providing sites and services," said the Director of Housing, in Trinidad Mr. Michael Fuentes.

According to the new book coming out from intensive research done by the Inter-American Development Bank (IDB), "Room for Development: Housing Markets in Latin America" currently there are one in three families in Latin America and the Caribbean, or 59 million people, living in dwellings that are either unsuitable for habitation or are built with poor materials and lacking basic infrastructure and services. Additionally, there are as many as 2 million persons who are forced to settle in informal housing, such as slums, and high risk areas because of an insufficient supply of adequate and affordable dwellings.

Many studies also suggest that governments should adopt housing policies that offer households greater flexibility to meet their housing needs, going beyond simply providing low-income families with outright housing grants or subsidies to buy houses.

Another option in the menu of public policies to reduce the region's housing gap is to foster the rental market for low-cost housing, paving the way for the creation of private enterprises specializing in rental units for the low-income population. That would help increase the supply of adequate and affordable dwellings and give this growing segment of the population greater flexibility to adapt to economic cycles since it will be easier for them to move to areas with better job prospects even if they do not own a house.

"There is no simple single solution to closing in the region's housing gap. Policies must offer households more and better choices: to rent or own; to move or stay; to borrow or not; to buy or build."

Essay by Edlin D. Rochford
2014

a. State the writer's main point
b. Write an ESSAY, in approximately 500 words, in which you include:
    (i) The writer's purpose
    (ii) The effectiveness of at least TWO organizational strategies and TWO language techniques that the writer used to achieve that purpose.

Total 25 mark

SECTION A
MODULE 1 – GATHERING and PROCESSING INFORMATION

Read the excerpt below and answer the questions that follow.

As she took her place at the back of the lectern she breathed deeply in an effort to calm the nervous shaking of her limbs and the tremors in her stomach. Debating was her passion and the topic of Forest fires was a lived experience but still she was nervous. Looking at the judges, Chairperson, time-keeper, members of the opposing side and finally the audience, she felt ready.

As a mere civilian, forest fires doing their yearly damage to the land both in the valleys and on the mountains never fail to distress me. I know from seeing the scope of the charred remains of what used to be lush green vegetation that the damage was bad but I truly didn't know that it was this bad.

Judges, Chairperson, time-keeper, members of the opposing side, audience ...Greetings! My name is Raquel Birsa and we, my partner Asia Mangaroo and I are here today to propose the motion, "Be it resolved that forests are man-made and not naturally caused."

People please picture this phenomenon! It's the beginning of March and the hills are covered in smoke and woe to the houses that are in close vicinity of these raging environment eating monsters. If perchance you forgot to ensure that all openings in your dwelling are tightly shut, then what your eyes will behold upon entry will be indeed a sight that could send shock waves into your very being. Soot, soot and more soot everywhere as there is no escaping of this unwelcomed invader.

I know that many persons in the Caribbean looked upon with fear and trepidation as the annual dry season approaches. And we know that uncontrolled blazes fuelled by the ignorance of humanity, weather, and wind, and dry underbrush, wildfires can burn acres of land—and consume everything in their paths—in mere minutes. And yet year after year, day after day, hour after hour the land is ablaze with what my partner and I could only describe as "the raging inferno of earthly hell on this place we call earth, our home."

Did you know that, according to the United Nations Food and Agriculture Organisation (FAO) global forest inventory in 2005, forests cover about 25 per cent of the region's terrestrial surface, totalling 5.87 million hectares (ha)? Whilst some of you may quickly think that this area represents only 0.1 per cent of the global forest cover to the Caribbean, many of us know that a substantial amount of it is damaged land.

In our research we found out that Dr Marcos Pedro Ramos Rodríguez a Fire Management Professor based at the Forestry and Agronomy Faculty of Pinar del Río University, Cuba published in his survey that during the period 1995 to 2003 in the four countries of Cuba, Dominica, Dominican Republic, Trinidad and Tobago, a total of **not 100, not 3000 but, listen to this 7,727 forest fires** were officially recorded. During this period in the countries of Cuba, Dominican Republic, Trinidad and Tobago the area burned in wild-land fires was about 150,000ha.

Now we know that there are plenty of natural phenomena that can turn the landscape into a blazing inferno and send wildlife and human beings fleeing to safety such as lightning, volcanoes and of course… dragons but these are in the minority especially in the Caribbean.

Everyone in this audience knows that human reckless behaviours such as out of control 'slash and burn' agricultural practices, hunters lighting areas to flush animals out of hiding places and careless tossing of cigarettes out of car windows are common ways in which forest fires can result. So why would we believe differently? Why would we come here this morning and listen to the other side tell us that man is not the cause?

In the United States on average, more than 100,000 wildfires, also called wild land fires or forest fires, clear 4 million to 5 million acres (1.6 million to 2 million hectares) of land in the U.S. every year. In recent years, wildfires have burned up to 9 million acres (3.6 million hectares) of land. A wildfire moves at speeds of up to 14 miles an hour (23 kilometres an hour), consuming everything—trees, brush, homes, even humans—in its path.

The development of this pan-Caribbean strategy to link to the Global Wild-land Fire Network (GWFN), established within the framework of the United Nations International Strategy for Disaster Reduction (UNISDR) is one major part of the efforts of the countries in the area to reduce this devastation.

In summary, if you leave here with nothing else we hope that you will leave with this Proverb, "Uncontrolled fire, uncontrolled water, and uncontrolled governments know nothing of mercy."

(i)   State the writer's main point.
Write an ESSAY, in approximately 500 words, in which you include:
(ii) The writer's purpose

(iii) The effectiveness of at least TWO organizational strategies and TWO language techniques that the writer used to achieve that purpose.

(iv) Identify and discuss TWO organizational strategies which lend validity and reliability to this information.

Composed by Edlin D. Rochford
2014

Total 25 marks

SECTION A
MODULE 1 – GATHERING and PROCESSING INFORMATION

Read the excerpt below and answer the questions that follow

Did you know that the majority, yes the majority of young people between the ages of 15-24 are HIV free? And do you know why? Well, it's certainly not because they are bombarded with "warnings about risky behaviour and HIV" and neither is it because of the dread of 'getting HIV' that some people are trying to put in them. Rather, despite of all that is lacking to treat with the issue of young people and HIV, the majority of young people are not indulging in risky behaviours and we are HIV free. Let's face it, it could have been worse! But it isn't!

According to Rodger Samuel, Minister of Social Development, statistics out of the office of the Prime Minister on May 1st 2013 only 3,500 youths from our population of 116 thousand young people are living with HIV.

This makes the number of young people who do not have HIV is in the majority and we would like to commend these young people who are HIV free.

Many persons sit and bash, criticize and rebuff young people because they believe that young people are wild that young people are careless and not heeding 'the warning'. But am I the only one, who is asking,

"What warning are they talking about?"
"Who's giving this warning?"
"Where are young people seeing or hearing this warning?"
How many billboards do you see with information warning young people about HIV?
Are these 'warnings' shown in movie theatres where young people hang out?

Nope but some people dare to criticize young people for not heeding "the warning and indulging in risky behaviours"

Well warnings we do not know about but, what we do know is that according to a report published on the **unaidscaribbean.org** website, "more than two decades into the epidemic, the vast majority of young people remain uninformed about sex and sexually transmitted infections (STIs). Although a majority have heard of AIDS, many do not know how HIV is spread and do not believe they are at risk. Those young people who do know something about HIV often do not protect themselves", "Have you ever wondered why this is so? Well, we believe that it's not because of what the naysayers say and no it's not because young people are promiscuous and careless. We believe that this is because young people lack the skills, the support or the means to adopt safe behaviours". Yes young people who fall prey to HIV in most instances lack the skills, the support and the means to protect themselves!

Despite the lack and in spite of the slow pace of support in the case of our situation in Trinidad and Tobago the majority of young people are HIV free. The same UN organization said that countries where the spread of HIV/AIDS is subsiding or even declining, it is because young people are given the tools like education and programs and the incentives (to run these programs) to adopt safe behaviours.

So if we are to get to where HIV is declining or subsiding then stakeholders and young people must be given the tools and the incentives right before "the warning" right?

So where is this warning coming from? If there is no conscious effort to put HIV and AIDS education in our school curriculum then how can you be warning us?

    a. State the speaker's main point
    b. Write an ESSAY, in approximately 500 words, in which you include:
        (i) The speaker's purpose
        (ii) The effectiveness of at least TWO organizational strategies and TWO language techniques that the speaker used to achieve that purpose.
        (iii) The overall tone of the piece

Total 25 marks

SECTION A
MODULE 1 – GATHERING and PROCESSING INFORMATION

Read the excerpt below and answer the questions that follow

On Tuesday January 15 2015 the Seismic Centre of The University of the West Indies expressed about the Caribbean region capability to treat with all the aftershocks of a major earthquake saying that whilst its aim was not to create panic and pandemonium it felt that it needed to create awareness once again that we in this region were long overdue for a great earthquake magnitude 8.0 earthquake, which if and when it occurs would have brought with it 32 times more energy than the Haiti event. In light of these sobering facts, it is imperative for the region to move expeditiously towards building resilience to such events.

Are we ready? Are you ready?

On Monday 18th May, 2015 at 3:59am Trinidad and Tobago's local time, an earthquake occurred in the Gulf of Paria, Trinidad. The event was located at 10.62°N and 61.51°W. The magnitude was 3.4 and the depth was 53km. It was reportedly felt in places as Maraval, Petit Valley and St. Augustine.

Are we ready? Is Trinidad and Tobago ready? Earthquake ready?

Four days later on Thursday 21st May, 2015 at 9:25am Trinidad and Tobago's local time, another earthquake occurred this time, north of Paria Peninsula. The activity was located at 11.24°N and 61.87°W. The quake's magnitude was 4.6 and its depth was 44km. It was reported felt widely in Trinidad and parts of Tobago and Grenada. Please note that these results were reviewed by a seismologist at the Seismic Research at the University of the West Indies

On Friday 22nd May 2015 the public was told in no uncertain terms to brace ourselves mentally, physically and any other way we can be cause the region—and possibly Trinidad and Tobago—were still "long overdue" for a "great earthquake" and that the population must catch up on preparedness, this warning came from Dr Joan Latchman, director of Seismic Research at the University of the West Indies. The public was also made aware of the fact that while the UWI Centre collaborates continuously with the relevant state agencies in an effort to be prepared in every possible way, it was imperative that all citizens take personal preparation seriously and start with the implementing in the home of a hazard bag and disaster education.

One of the major reasons for such strict warning may be as a result of the fact that major earthquake disasters around the world have stimulated similar shifts and resulted in greater resilience to seismic hazards in these regions

Doing the relevant research one will see that according to the same University of the West Indies Seismic Research Centre 2014 report the Caribbean region including Trinidad and Tobago, Grenada, Antigua and Barbuda, Dominica, St. Lucia, Guadeloupe and Anguilla experienced 28 earthquakes, and for 2015 thus far there have been, 4 earthquakes reported in the Caribbean.

Has this alarming information change people's attitude towards disasters? Has it, for example stopped Trinidadians from foolishly or naively believing that "God is ah Trini" and has it shaken Jamaicans from their fear to leave their homes and worldly possessions and flee to safety? I guess one will have to just wait and see what their reaction will be in the face of the long overdue great earthquake. In the interim stakeholders are speaking out about what needs to be done in preparation and education.

One stakeholder group suggested that each country by way of its government and relevant ministries must develop, legislate and enforce stricter Building Codes using up-to-date seismic hazard maps that are based on the latest available science and technology. A second watchdog organization sought to emphasise that preparedness measures at the individual levels were insufficient and greater efforts were needed to facilitate self-resilience if Caribbean countries and by extension their citizens were to escape Haiti's 2010, 7.0 magnitude earthquake experience.

Just two reminders for those who are inclined to brush off warnings of these as doom and gloom, on October 21, 1766 at 10:65 St Joseph, Trinidad and Tobago was destroyed by a 7.9 earthquake. On Tuesday 12 January 2010, survivors of Haiti's quake described abject panic — much of it well-founded, as buildings imploded around them. Many Haitians grabbed cement pillars only to watch them crumble in their hands. Is this what we really want?

This is a quake up call Caribbean countries. Heed it!

    (i)   State the writer's main point.
Write an ESSAY, in approximately 500 words, in which you include:
    (ii)   The writer's DOMINANT purpose

(iii) The effectiveness of at least TWO organizational strategies and TWO language techniques that the writer used to achieve that purpose.

(iv) Identify and discuss TWO organizational strategies which lend validity and reliability to this information.

Completed by Edlin D. Rochford
2014

SECTION A
MODULE 1 – GATHERING and PROCESSING INFORMATION

Read the excerpt below and answer the questions that follow

Is Going Green Good for the Environment?

I guess because we are the opposing side to this motion everyone expects us to come here and say something like…we believe that going green is bad for the economy and we can prove it…well sorry to disappoint you…because no one in their right mind can say out right that going green is bad for the economy…it would be foolhardy of us to trivialize the benefits of going green but what we are here to strongly oppose to this notion that it is easy to go green…that we should blindly trust the process without questioning or knowing the process…that going green is the salvation of this planet…that there is nothing ulterior to going green…we are here to say yes going green is good but….I repeat going green is good for the economy but…yes it's these buts…that we are here to present to you.

Please permit me to define two terms in the motion

According to the prestigious Harvard Business Review published in August 2013, '… going **green** involves a lifestyle change, which could impact what car you drive, the bags you use for groceries and even the clothes you wear. Going green it continued is about buying local produce versus buying exotic foreign foods. Going green is as simple as choosing to buy recycled paper!'

On the other hand, our term of reference when we use the term economy comes from economy. com and refers to thrifty, frugal or stingy use of material resources as a means of economizing or saving.

Our first point is really in the form of a question…Are they selfish or not?

Shopping online is the latest craze in this country, people's taste for all things foreign has always been there because of our colonial past and the culture of dependency that was deliberately created and fostered but in the last 5 years it has magnified and so much so that local businesses according to local Chamber of Commerce Chairperson Alexandria Kanton, "small local businesses are experiencing the fall outs in terms of downsizing and decrease in profits all because of the online buying competition faced."

Let face it who can fault a person for exercising personal choice? We conducted a random survey in our community in which we gave 70 persons the definitions for both 'economy' and 'going green.' They were asked to respond to the questions. "If these are the criteria for online shopping, would you follow them? 50 out of the 70 persons (72%) said "No they would not" and their reasons ranged from:

1. I worked for my money and I should be able to spend it on what I want
2. We are a democracy right? This sounds like Cuba under Castro.
3. Nobody will tell me how to spend my money and on what to spend it on!

Would you want to change the lifestyle you have worked hard to maintain? How many of you are sticklers for taking the economy and the environment into serious consideration? Not many of us, but don't feel too badly because that is the second point we are here to make!

Many of us do not put the environment first!

Going green is good for the economy we cannot deny that but as individuals we are selfish and many of us will agree with the words of Napoleon Hill author and motivational speaker "Great achievement is usually born of great sacrifice, and is never the result of selfishness." The truth is few persons are ready to make great sacrifice in the effort of going green.

a. State the writer's main point in approximately 30 words.
b. Write an ESSAY, in approximately 500 words, in which you include:
   (i) The speaker's purpose
   (ii) The effectiveness of at least TWO organizational strategies and TWO language techniques that the speaker used to achieve that purpose.

Total 25 marks

SECTION A
MODULE 1 – GATHERING and PROCESSING INFORMATION

Read the excerpt below and answer the questions that follow

So you believe that only man and man alone is responsible for the global warming phenomenon? So you smirk at any idea that nature in its creative mode can conjure up the heat that is melting the polar ice? We are not here to deny that man's actions well intentioned or not may have a hand in exacerbating global warming but we categorically deny that global warming is solely as a result of man and has nothing to do with being a natural phenomenon. To believe this in its entirety is to put the burden squarely on the shoulders of man. We say here today that both men, indeed all of us and nature are responsible for the phenomenon of global warming.

According to the English Oxford dictionary, 'global warming is a gradual increase in the overall temperature of the earth's atmosphere generally attributed to the greenhouse effect caused by increased levels of carbon dioxide, cfcs and other pollutants.'

The term "man made" according to the Merriam Webster dictionary, is caused by human beings' and the term "natural" means that it is existing or derived from nature.

According to the World Health Organisation, global warming can be caused by the emission of green house gases such as carbon dioxide, methane and nitrous oxide into the environment.

Carbon dioxide, methane and nitrous oxide can be all produced both naturally and through human. For example methane can be produced by natural wetlands, agricultural activities and fuel extraction. Nitrous oxide on the other hand can be produced through agricultural activities and natural biological processes and finally natural sources of carbon dioxide include decomposition and natural sources come from activities such as deforestation

Research done by climate scientists from the EPA (United States Environmental Protection Agency) shows us that many factors both natural and manmade causes change in the earth's climate.

Scientists have pieced together a picture of the earth's climate, dating back to hundreds of thousands of years by analyzing a number of increased climates.

The historical record shows that the climate system varies naturally over a wide range of time scales. In general, climate change prior to the industrial revolution in the 1700s can be explained by natural causes such as solar energy, volcanic eruptions, natural changes in the green house gas concentrations etc.

Recent climate changes, however, cannot be explained by natural causes alone. Various studies indicate that natural causes are likely to explain some of the observed changes especially since the mid 20th century. Human activities have also contributed to global warming.

So, why do some people want to believe that only man or only nature has to have a hand in this? Why is there this tendency to want things either black or white? When we know that life is made up of various shades of grey! Is it just because that most persons focus on the negatives of global warming they want us to believe that it's man made? Well equally there are many persons who are saying that global warming is both as a result of nature and the actions of man.

a. State the writer's main point in approximately 30 words.
b. Write an ESSAY, in approximately 500 words, in which you include:
    (i)   The speaker's purpose
    (ii) The effectiveness of at least TWO organizational strategies and TWO language techniques that the speaker used to achieve that purpose.

Total 25 marks

14. STUDENTS' ACTIVITY #3: **MAIN POINT AND DOMINANT PURPOSE**

The following Main Ideas are from Module One Past Papers. After reading the extracts, your task is to write a sentence that reflects the DOMINANT Purpose of the writer.

Main Point -The University of The West Indies is adding an online 'fourth campus' to become more accessible, partly because of competition, and to produce 'work-ready' graduates.
Purpose-
Main Point -There is no factual basis for the superstition that deaths increase in leap years.
Purpose-
Main Point -Tsunamis are vast, speedy, high energy bodies of far travelling seawater that can wreak havoc on coastal areas.
Purpose-
Main Point -Most of the information that is presented during news broadcasts is primarily about trivial issues aimed at simply attracting viewers.
Purpose-
Main Point -Women and men have polarized views when it comes to relationships.
Purpose-
Main Point -To praise/welcome/approve of UWI's initiative to open an online fourth campus while cautioning against complacency in the face of continuing competition.
Purpose-
Main Point -Hybrid cars have many advantages over gasoline powered cars and potential buyers need to have a good understanding of how they work.
Purpose-
Main Point -Having wasted their primary and secondary academic opportunities, both male and female young adults in the workplace, are frustratingly illiterate and innumerate.
Purpose-
Main Point -Education is the only option that women have for breaking free from the stranglehold that illiteracy has over them as manifested in their personal health, education, and economic, social and political opportunities.
Purpose-

ACROSS

2. The consistency of your measurement or the degree to which an instrument measures the same way each time it is used under the same condition with the same subjects.
3. These sources are documents that are created at or near the time or situation being researched.
4. This method can happen on a range of observer and participant relationships.
5. In statistics includes all members of a defined group that we are studying
8. A writer can choose a mixture of different organizational strategies and language techniques to achieve this.
12. Repeating the initial consonant of a group of words for aural effect and memorability
13. Comprehension questions that often ask for details the writer has provided as support
14. The general and broad content of a research paper.
15. The result of processing, gathering, manipulating and or organizing data in a way that adds to the knowledge of the receiver.
16. Someone with experience, qualification and expertise.
17. This question is asked at this level of comprehension; how will the information in this article be useful to you?
18. The specific issue being discussed in your Portfolio.
19. A systematic process of collecting or gathering and analyzing data and information
20. They are generally a gathering of 8 to 12 persons who came together to discuss a selected topic of interest that is relevant to the research that is being undertaken.

DOWN

1. Introduction, conclusion, logical linkages, editing and revising.
6. This is concerned with the success at measuring what was set out to be measured.
7. These can be sent out or administered by post, face to face, by telephone or even via the internet
9. Trying to impress or influence by overstating a viewpoint, statement or idea.
10. Can refer to facts, figures, numbers, text images or words, sounds that are obtained from experiments, observations or a set of premises.
11. Illustrations, Historical data and Facts, Statistical data are all examples of these.

16. STUDENTS' ACTIVITY #5: **CROSSWORD REVIEW #2 OF MODULE ONE**

ACROSS

2. The samples that are used in research are found in this
4. When you comprehend at this level you look for the factual information
6. Someone who has the qualifications and the experience is considered an
8. This contains all the rules that you are expected to know in Standard English
9. Descriptive, expository, argumentative discourses are all literary
11. Although, therefore, however, additionally are all
13. You, your teacher and your friends may do this
15. Periods, question marks, commas, and exclamation marks

DOWN

1. This is information that you get from people who were not there when the event took place
3. To summarise your notes in a specific order
5. Another way of communicating in both the oral and written form
7. The extent to which your findings are consistent and accurate over time
10. When you focus on listening and reading, you are at this comprehension level
12. Your Primary sources in a census will all provide
14. Is your research measuring what you set out to measure?

SECTION B

17.   THE FORMAT OF MODULE TWO ESSAY QUESTION IN PAPER 02

In Module Two essay students are asked to read an extract containing one or more language situations and respond by discussing statements like the following:

In an essay of no more than 500 words, discuss the following:

a) What the poet achieves by using a mixture of Standard English and Creole in the poem
b) The implication for the wider acceptability of Creole arising from the poet's use of this language variety
c) How a video presentation would enhance the message of the poem

NB: Remember that the number and the focus of the statements vary according to the language situation of the excerpt.

Total 25 marks

18. FACTORS TO CONSIDER WHEN WRITING MODULE TWO ESSAYS

NB: - The excerpt that is given will look and read like a Literature or Language Arts piece and there is nothing wrong with reading it as such BUT keep in mind that you are doing Communication Studies and so remember to look for the factors that must be considered when writing Module 2 essay such as: *[language, registers, content, context, audience and all its demographics, perceptions (personal or society's), purpose, historical past, personal choice]*

Language (Always identify if the language used is the Standard or the Creole being used)

A person may choose either language type 'appropriately' or 'inappropriately' whilst taking these factors into consideration:

- ➤ register you wish to create
- ➤ content you wish to put across
- ➤ audience you are interacting with
- ➤ the context in which the situation is taking place

Register (identify which type which you wish to create, which language you will use to do so, what audience that you are interacting with, the content you wish to put across, the context in which the situation is taking place) **Registers** are always **created** never **used** because of these factors:

- ➤ language used
- ➤ audience involved
- ➤ content
- ➤ context

Content (your topic, your message) what you are going to speak about influences the language that you are going to eventually choose.

Context (where, what, and the audience involved) where you are interacting influences your language choice and register. The reason for the interaction also influences your language choice and the register. The audience that you are interacting with also influence your language choice and register.

Audience (the people involved directly in the situation) the demographics of your audience influence the language that you choose and the register that is created. When interacting with any audience or mixed audience, pay attention to these factors:

➤ the age or ages
➤ their status
➤ their occupation
➤ where they lived

Purpose (reason for the situation or the interaction) then your choice of language is dependent on the purpose or the reason for the interaction.

➤ Are you interacting to entertain?
➤ Are you interacting to inform?

Perception about language (not always do people choose their language because of perception but sometimes they do) perception is always influenced by:

➤ personal beliefs about the language in question
➤ what other persons have influenced you to believe
➤ or what the society has dictated as the norm

19. SUGGESTIONS FOR WRITING YOUR BEST MODULE TWO ESSAYS - USING THE "PEE" FORMAT FOR MODULE TWO ESSAY

For your introduction:

You may look at what you are asked to discuss and summarize it as an introduction.

BUT

Do not get carried away! Your introduction is just pointing the direction! So be **brief!**

After your brief introduction you may begin to use the PEE format.

P-make a general **Point** or broad or general statement about whatever topic you are asked to discuss. A general statement may begin like this, **"Most poets use a mixture of the Standard and Creole to…"**

E-give an appropriate **Example** from the extract that will support the point that you made

For Module Two essay, just like Module One, the Example that you use must be taken from the given extract. Do not write line number but write out the example. You may use Ellipsis **only** if you know how to use it correctly otherwise as I have cautioned my students, for safety sake, please write out the example that supports your **Point**.

E-give an **Explanation**

For Module Two essay the Explanation should be justifying or giving reason or reasons for the Point that you made. Your explanation by way of justification or reason must be sound. An explanation may sound like this: - **It is possible that this poet in question is speaking to a mixed audience who understands and is comfortable with both languages. An example of this can be seen in …**

Very importantly before you begin to explain or justify your responses, please identify or name what you are going to write about! For example if the question asks you about the language (or tone, context, and register) used by the author or the characters, then the first thing you need to do is identify the language or tone or context or register. Some students just jump right in and begin to write about "the language", "the tone", "the" context", "the register" but they never identify what language or tone or context or register they are writing about. For example the language may be either Creole English or Standard English or any named Caribbean Creole or Standard English, the tone may be critical, the context may be in a hairdressing salon and the register may be casual. Your main objective here is to be specific!

20. SOME TRANSITION OR LINKING WORDS

generally speaking	However
Consequently	On the other hand
clearly, then	Nevertheless
furthermore	On the contrary
Additionally	In this situation

21. MARKING SCHEME WITH ALLOCATION OF MARKS FOR MODULE TWO ESSAY

Content – **10 marks**

(a)   Award marks for attention to **ANY** of the following points:

Award **4 marks** for coverage and discussion of 3 or more points
Award **3 marks** for coverage and discussion of 2 points
Award **2 marks** for coverage and discussion of 1 point
Award **1 mark** for vague coverage of points

(b)   Award **3 marks** for this section OR
Award **1 mark** for **EACH** of any **THREE** correct responses

(c)   Award **3 marks** for this section OR
Award **1 mark** for **EACH** of any **THREE** correct responses

CONTENT = 10 marks (a=2 + b=2+ c=6) or (a=4+b=3+c=3)

- A superior response that addresses ALL areas identified **9-10 marks**
- A good response that addresses most of the areas identified **3 – 8 marks**
- A fair response that addresses half of the areas identified, but not fully developed **5 – 6**
- A weak response- less than half of expected content. Not well developed. **3 – 4**
- A poor response – Minimal content evident **0-3**

Organization	7
Excellent introduction, thematic cohesion in paragraphs, appropriate use of transitional devices, effective conclusion.	7
Good use of the above with one to two weaknesses.	5-6
Adequate level of organization with several weaknesses noted.	3-4
Unsatisfactory level of organization. Weaknesses in all areas identified above.	1-2

Expression	8
Excellent, effective and error-free use of language.	8
Very good use of language though there may be a few lapses.	7
Good use of language though there may be a few lapses.	5-6
Some ability to use language accurately and effectively, but with some inconsistency in accurate usage.	3-4
Frequent, inaccurate use of language. **OR** Insufficient information presented.	1-2
Inability to use language accurately. **OR** Too little information presented to make an assessment.	0

Remember: Paper 02 is not a short answer paper but it is an essay/discussion paper. If you look closely at the mark scheme for each section you will notice that you will be given marks for all these elements that make up an excellent essay such as **language, introduction, thematic cohesion** in paragraphs, appropriate use of **transitional devices** and effective **conclusion**.

22. STUDENTS' ACTIVITY #6: **THE RIGHT VIEW OR THE WRONG VIEW**

The box contains some right and wrong views that people have about language. Differentiate the right from the wrong view.

	PEOPLE'S VIEWS	RIGHT or WRONG
1.	Some people believe that non-standard dialects are not simply offshoots from the standard.	

2.	Some people believe that the standard dialect is the "correct" way to speak the language.	
3.	Some people believe that what is considered standard is to be only associated with prestige	
4.	Some people believe that the non-standard language is more complex, more logical, and more expressive than the standard dialects.	
5.	Some people believe that languages have various dialects.	
6.	Some people believe that there are actually a range of varieties that people consider to be standard.	
7.	Some people believe that dialects are a product of **"lazy"** speech.	
8.	Some people believe that from a linguistic standpoint, what is considered standard has nothing to do with correctness or superiority.	
9.	Some people believe that from a linguistic standpoint, all dialects are equally correct, equally expressive, equally complex and equally logical.	
10.	Some people believe that a language is composed of a "standard" dialect from which all of the other non-standard dialects emerge	
11.	Some people believe that the term non-standard dialect means just that, *not the standard dialect*. It does not mean inferior or sub-standard.	
12.	Some people believe that other dialects represent erroneous or inferior ways of speaking the language	
13.	Some people believe that non-standard and standard dialects taken together simply make up the range of dialects that constitute a language.	

23. STUDENTS' GROUP ACTIVITY #7: **WORKING IN GROUPS OF 4, DISCUSS THESE QUESTIONS.**

1. What reasons are there for using or choosing a specific language, Creole or Standard?
2. What are the factors which may influence a person's choice of language?
3. What are some factors which would motivate a person to choose a specific language?
4. Which language is being used here? Is it the Standard? Or is it the Creole?

5. Where is the person? Look at the setting or the context.
6. What is the topic of discussion?
7. In our Caribbean situation, when do we mainly use the Standard?
8. In our Caribbean situation, when do we mainly use the Creole?
9. Why do we choose the Standard over the Creole in a specific situation?
10. Who are the speakers or members of the audience involved in this situation?
11. What are the feelings or attitudes or beliefs accompanying a person's choice of language?
12. What does the society think about Creole or Standard?
13. Is there a belief that there are specific instances or contexts where Creole is deemed appropriate?
14. Is there a belief that there are specific instances or contexts where Creole is deemed inappropriate?
15. Is there a belief that there are specific instances or contexts where the Standard is deemed appropriate?
16. Is there a belief that there are specific instances or contexts where the Standard is deemed inappropriate?
17. Does your country's historical past influence your language (Creole and Standard) situation?
18. What issues arise from the fact that we have an official and an unofficial language?
19. What are the linguistic and non-linguistic factors that influence a person's choice of language?
20. What are some non- linguistic factors that lead a non-native speaker to believe that he/she knows a new language?
21. What are some linguistic factors that a non-native speaker needs to understand in order to obtain command of a new language?

24. SOME SUGGESTIONS FOR RESPONSES TO MODULE TWO ESSAY DISCUSSION TOPICS IN CAPE PAST PAPERS

Discussion topic - Factors which may lead writers/poets/authors to use Creole in their work.

➢ A person's choice of Creole in the production of their literary piece may be influenced by many factors, for example for the author Michael Anthony it may be possible that

- Creole is his first language/native/mother tongue

- The topic is best understood/delivered in Creole
- The topic is a close and an emotional one
- The author knows another language but uses Creole to show that he is proud of his heritage, in this case Creole is used as his identity marker
- By using Creole he is making a very strong case in support of Creole being a language as any other language

NB: Any of these may be an answer but only after you have read the passage/poem and have understood the context

Discussion topic - Factors which may have motivated a character to lapse into Creole (this Creole may be Trinidadian/Jamaican or any other country's) to comfort another character

➤ The word lapse here implies that these characters also speak a second language

- There are many possible factors which may motivate a character to lapse into Creole in an attempt to comfort another character. It is possible that Creole is their first language and as such it is not uncommon for persons when experiencing some kind of emotional upheaval to revert to their first/mother tongue.
- Whenever persons who are bi-lingual or speak 2 languages become positively or negatively emotional they tend to revert to their first language
- Sometimes the Creole is the better/more appropriate of the two languages to convey what the situation calls for. Many persons perceive French Creole or Patois as a language of comfort.

Discussion topic - When a character /writer/poet uses a specific language i.e. Creole or the Standard in a specific situation, what does he/she hope to achieve?

- Sometimes a character uses a specific language to be accepted as a citizen of that country
- Wants to reach that specific audience
- Or to show that this language is a language as in the case of Creole

➤ The reasons for a (named person's) use of any specific Caribbean Creole

- It's the person's first language and therefore he or she is comfortable using it.

- The context is appropriate for the use of Creole. Traditionally Creole is used in casual or informal contexts but language is always a personal choice and one may choose to be unconventional and speak Creole in a formal context.
- The audience understands Creole (Creole speaking audience).
- Creole is appropriate for the theme or topic (appropriate context).

Discussion topic - Factors which may have influenced the writer's (speaker's, poet's, author's, journalist's etc) choice of language

NB: The first thing we do here is to identify and name the language. Is it the Standard or is it Creole?

Choice of one's language is influenced by factors such as

- The target audience's ability to understand the Standard or the Creole.
- The writer is familiar with the target audience.
- The context in which the language is used is conventionally appropriate.
- The language is appropriate for the content that is being shared. Conventionally Creole is used for less serious matters, for telling stories and entertaining. Standard on the other hand, is usually used for official business, academic writing etc

Discussion topic - The suitability or appropriateness of a person's use of Jamaican English Creole (could be substituted for Trinidadian, Grenadian, Barbadian etc) in a specific context

- Identify the context.
- Is the language choice suitable for this specific context?
- If so, then give reason(s) to justify or if not, then also give reason(s) to justify.

Discussion topic - The implications for the wider acceptability of Creole arising from the poet's use of this language variety

- Traditionally Creole is either accepted or not accepted.
- The use of Creole as a literary tool contributes further to the acceptability
- When Creole is accepted it's because of the audience's positive beliefs about Creole
- Implications for acceptability speaks of accessing the material, even understanding the material, taking ownership of the language that is used (in this case Creole)

- The use of Creole reflects societal use of Creole also
- By publishing that use in a work of art she is celebrating the societal usage and, in particular, lifting the credibility of Creole.
- Is the reader proud of the language? Pride leads to acceptability.
- Having a positive attitude or perception of the language invariably leads to wider acceptability.
- Her usage gives the impression that one language is not better suited than the other for the expression of her message; that, indeed, one can code switch.
- May lead to more writers using it as a credible literary tool in published literary works
- Will lead to the development of an orthography for this Creole language
- Will lead to more formal application in education
- Higher probability of research into different genres in Creole
- May lead to the inclusion of Creole in a national language policy

Discussion topic - A person's attitude to Creole or to Standard English or attitude to language

- Students who speak Creole or dialect or a non-standard language are criticized for speaking it
- They are taught to abandon Creole and learn the Standard, at least for educational purposes.
- They are told that they should speak the Standard in order to maximize their success opportunities in examinations.
- A command of the Standard helps them in their quest for tertiary education and well paid employment.
- A command of the Standard ensures upward social mobility.

Discussion topic - What is the relationship between language choice and context? What other factors influence language choice?

- Audience with all the demographics that come with it (age, social status, gender, educational background, relationship with speaker) always influence language choice
- Content –what you have to say **can** influence your language choice
- Context – where you are saying it? What's the occasion? These are the contexts that influence language choice.

Discussion topic - What is the relationship between registers and context? What other factors influence registers?

- Registers are created and influenced by your language choice, content, context and audience (with all its demographics)
- Creole language is often times associated with the casual or informal and intimate registers and likewise the Standard is the opposite.
- The formal register that's created by serious, academic, legal document and content are often times written in the Standard language.
- Friends, loved ones, family and peers together always create registers that are casual and intimate in nature. The language often times used is Creole.

Discussion topic - What factors may lead to a speaker using a mixture of 2 languages?

- Mixing 2 languages can be seen as code-switching. Why would a speaker code-switch? Janet Holmes says on the issue of code-switching according to the topic when she says, *'people may switch code within a speech event to discuss a particular topic'* (Holmes, 2000).
- For example, a Caribbean English bilingual will most likely talk about memories in the Caribbean in Creole or her native tongue since her emotional, nostalgic experiences may trigger her to speak in her native tongue.
- Code-switching can be used by speakers to express certain feelings and attitudes. Bi-lingual speakers may switch codes to express happiness, excitement, anger, sadness, and many other feelings.
- Speakers' code-switch in persuasion and rhetoric because they feel that they will grab their audience's attention and be more capable of achieving her/his goal. Code-switching also reflects a certain socioeconomic identity which can give the speaker a level of credibility and reliability.
- A speaker may mix her languages even if she is at home. Why? Because of these 3 factors: audience (with all its demographics), context and content.
- Reasons for migration vary from individual to individual, so why would a speaker in a foreign land mix her languages? Because she has lived there long enough to have a command of the language and can therefore mix her languages comfortably when needs be because of audience, content and context.

Discussion topic - What does a poet or writer or speaker or person achieve by using a mixture of languages?

- Connection with his/her audience as they will grab their audience's attention whether at home or abroad and be more capable of achieving his/her goal.
- Achieves a level of credibility and reliability through this connection.

Discussion topic - What does language reveal about the nature of a relationship or a situation?

- Language, whether Creole or Standard reveals things about relationships. For example people who are close or intimate often times speak to each other in the dialect or Creole, not worrying to stick to the conventions of the Standard all the time. They may even code-switch. The situation is very relaxed.
- The opposite can be said of the Standard which is often times used in situations like the workplace, between client and provider and persons who are older and younger.

Discussion topic - Analysis of a context and its effect on the language behaviour (what's another name for this term?) of characters

- Just as authors must choose what to say, they must also choose how to say it. The choice of content and language are closely related. Choices of content and language reflect and reinforce each other.
- Whenever you are asked about context you need to consider where the situation is taking place or the setting? With whom or the audience and all its demographics? Is it with a group, intrapersonal, organization etc?
- Contexts influence what we say and how we say it. Think about this in terms of the questions above.

Discussion topic - Character's interpretation of and reaction to another person's non-verbal gestures

- There are non-verbal gestures that make you feel comfortable and nice and then there are non-verbal gestures that make you feel downright uncomfortable, upset and angry.

- You have to remember though, because its non-verbal gestures that you are treating with there is always a measure of ambiguity that can lead not only to different interpretations but also to misinterpretation and ultimately the wrong reaction on the part of the character.

Discussion topic - What is *'good'* expression and what do people hope to achieve by using 'good' expression?

- In the Caribbean we have a history of associating *'good'* expression or language with the Standard language. The Standard is always the language of the colonizers.
- Persons using the Standard or *'good'* expression always hope to be perceived as:
    - Intelligent having attended a *'prestige'* school and university
    - Well travelled
    - Better than the other person or on the same level with them
    - Having achieved upward social mobility

Discussion topic - How can behaviour reveal one person's attitude to another's choice of language?

- Context – Principal's office
    - **Taryn,** *"Sir is jus dat ah did have to baby sit mih baby sista, yuh understan'?"*
    - **Principal standing straight,** *"Young lady, you are in Upper 6 aren't you? And you have completed five years of compulsory Language Arts, haven't you?"*
- What does the Principal's behaviour reveal about Taryn's language choice? His sarcasm at her language is obvious.

Discussion topic - What are the different ways that people use language?

- ➢ People use language in different ways and for different reasons:

    - For survival functions: Meeting your most basic needs
    - Social functions: Interacting with other people
    - For socializing
    - For establishing and maintaining relationships
    - To put up barriers
    - To influence people

- To give feedback
- When involved in an argument
- To avoid trouble
- To express oneself
- When expressing opinions
- To express emotions
- For cognitive functions
- When managing conversations

Discussion topic - What are the social factors that may account for person's language choice?

- Language is a social factor.
- Language is a distinguishing element
- The languages of developed societies - let's call it Civilization - all distinguish between more and less refined or elevated speech.
- Whether a speaker is educated will be obvious from his speech, and his economic status, geographical and ethnic background may also be deduced.
- A person's political affiliation inevitably infects the language.
- Most times West Indians children struggle with saying words that the older generation used.
- Language affects social behaviour.
- Social factors may affect your language, depending on your status in society, for example if you are poor and cannot afford an education or you were raised to believe schooling wasn't important or you grew up in a rural area where the Standard wasn't encouraged, your way of speaking might be different or not as eloquent as opposed to someone of higher standing.

Discussion topic - Differences and similarities between two persons' speech types or language codes

➤ **Which speech types or language codes are you to consider?**

- There are similarities and there are differences between the Standard and the Creole language codes that we use in our individual communities.
- Similarities and differences are identified in grammar, phonology and vocabulary

- Responses for this question can be found in your syllabus in Module 2 : Language and Community.

Discussion topic - What are possible factors that can indicate a person's social status?

- Language
- Address for home and work
- School and university they attended
- Profession
- Vehicle they drive (optional)
- Their dress code and artefacts e.g. jewellery
- Their friends and associates

Possible reasons for the writer's language choices used in the narrative?

N.B The question is asking for language (not registers) choices (plural not singular)
N.B Remember that language is used and register is created!
N.B There is no such thing as a casual or a Formal language nor is there "broken and bad" language
N.B The question asked for possible reasons and so you MUST give reasons for the writer's use of Creole and Standard English

- Identify immediately the two languages; Creole (or you may be more specific with Basilect, Mesolect) and Acrolect or just Creole and Standard English.
- Creole for the narration and Acrolect for the dialogue between the Archdeacon or Basilect/Mesolect for the narration and Acrolect for the dialogue.
- Creole is the major medium used in this instance to create comedic effect.
- Additionally, if a possible reason is "Creole enhances the comedic effect", then the opposite must be a reason for using the Standard English (i.e. the use of Standard English enhances the seriousness of the situation"
- The languages of the text show appreciation to the existence of an audience (in the Caribbean) of different varieties.
- The languages of the text reflect varieties of language as used in the Caribbean.
- Characters' social rank reflects or determines their language choice
- A character's level of education or exposure to education is reflected in language choice

- A character might choose to speak in Standard English in recognition of the high position of the other speaker in the dialogue.

Be careful and not do these things!

1. Do not write the literary analysis required for Module 1, where you actually identify contexts of communication and literary devices.
2. Do not do the language analysis that the IA required, where you focus on the features of communicative behaviours, registers, attitudes to language and dialectal variation without linking them to the questions and your subsequent responses.
3. Do not, not identify the language choices made in the passage, even though this was not asked in the question. This will inevitably result in a loss, as the mark scheme requires you to specifically state the languages chosen, in order to get the marks for any reasons you theorize.
4. Do not regurgitate only notes without applying it to the information in the passage.

Difficulties that non–West Indians may experience in understanding the passage?

- Lack of understanding of some Creole syntax, for example: Tenseless descriptions of events (non–West Indians will not have an idea of when the event took place)
- Non West Indians will not understand Creole lexical terms, for example, "screwing up her face" and "stopped braps"
- Non–West Indians will experience difficulties in understanding the lack of pluralisation of nouns
- Non–West Indians will experience difficulties in understanding the Creole habit of using onomatopoeic words as adverbs, for example, "braps"

Be careful to write a clear explanation and examples from the piece to support.
Remember that attitude to language must not be the deciding factor UNLESS there is clear indication or mention of this in the passage.

How a video presentation could enhance the comedic effect of the passage?
NB: For every response you have chosen you must ask yourself this question, "Will this create a comedic effect? In other words will there laughter over this response?" If the answer is 'no' then your response is incorrect.

- Your responses must have accompanying examples from the passage and an explanation as to how this example may be deemed comedic.

Be careful not to just mention things like stage directions, dress, artefact, and communicative behaviours without ensuring that these can create comedic effect. If it cannot then it is not an answer!

Discussion topic - How a televised presentation could help readers to understand character's attitudes?

- We understand attitudes by paying attention to what the person is saying, how she/he is saying it, what he/she is doing, how he/she is doing it.
- Attitude can be understood by seeing, hearing and interpreting words and actions of the person.
- Sometimes we hear something but we do not see the person and therefore we cannot come to a complete understanding.
- Television gives us the opportunity to see and hear the character looking at facial expression, gestures, body movements, clothes they are wearing.
- Even seeing the setting on the television helps us to view the character in a different light.

Discussion topic - How a televised presentation could enhance understanding of the situation in the excerpt?

NB: Always have EXAMPLES from the passage to support your answers! No examples from the passage will get you no marks!

- The language of video and television appeals to the sensibility of the audience population, whose communication results from the meeting point among words, gestures and movements, colours, sounds thus separating it from the linearity and static of the written word. Video and television are dynamic, and are directed to the affectivity of the audience. Give an example from the passage!
- The video medium can be sensorial, visual, spoken language, musical and written language. Languages that interact interconnected, added together, not separated, that's the strength of videos. Give an example from the passage!

- The audio visuals hit all our senses and in many ways. They persuade us, inform, entertain, project in other realities (the imaginary) and in other times and spaces. Give an example from the passage!
- The video combines the kinaesthetic-sensorial communication with the audiovisual, the intuition with the logics, and the emotion with the reason. It does so, but it starts from the sensorial, from the emotional and the intuitive to reach later the reasoning. Give an example from the passage!
- Video presentation will highlight the symbols of the message found in the excerpt. Give an example from the passage!
- Video presentation allows us to closely understand what is portrayed in the body language and facial expressions of the actors. Give an example from the passage!
- Video presentations allow viewers to hear the contrasting tones of the actors' voices. Give an example from the passage!
- The video will use body language, facial expressions and statements of the actors to evoke feelings from the audience. Give an example from the passage!
- A video presentation will enhance your work especially in the area of clearing up "grey" or "fuzzy" words, phrases and situations. Give an example from the passage!
- You are able to produce a variety of situations, voices and accents. Give an example from the passage!
- Listeners can now see the presentation instead of having to only visualize. Give an example from the passage!
- Camera alters the meaning of the situation as you can now see so much more things that you will use to understand. Give an example from the passage!

25.   STUDENTS' ACTIVITY #8: **MODULE TWO ESSAY QUESTIONS REVIEW**

1	THREE reasons for a person's use of Trinidadian Creole
A	
B	
C	
2	Factors which may have influenced the writer's (speaker's, poet's, author's, journalist's) choice of language
A	
B	
C	
3	The suitability or appropriateness of a person's use of Jamaican English Creole in a specific context.
A	
B	
C	
4	The implications for the wider acceptability of a chosen language (Which of the 2 languages would need to be accepted?). In other words can this language be widely accepted and why?
A	
B	
C	
5	The factors which may have motivated a person or persons to lapse into another language?
A	
B	
C	
6	A person's attitudes to Creole or to Standard English. [Where do they originate and what might they be?]
A	
B	
C	
7	What is the relationship between language choice and context? What other factors influence language choice?
A	

B	
C	
8	What is the relationship between registers and context? What other factors influence registers?
A	
B	
C	
9	What factors may lead to a speaker using a mixture of 2 languages?
A	
B	
C	
10	What does a poet or writer or speaker or person achieves by using a mixture of languages?
A	
B	
C	
11	What does language reveal about the nature of a relationship or a situation? Give examples to support.
A	
B	
C	
12	Analysis of a context and its effect on the language behaviour of characters. What is another way to write this?
A	
13	Character's interpretation of and reaction to another person's non-verbal gestures [Support with examples]
A	
B	
C	
14	What is 'good' expression and what do people hope to achieve by using 'good' expression?
A	
B	
C	
15	How can behaviour reveal one person's attitude to another's choice of language?
A	

B	
C	
16	What are the different ways that persons use language?
A	
B	
C	
17	What are the social factors that may account for person's language choice?
A	
B	
C	
18	Differences and similarities between two persons' speech types
A	
B	
C	
19	How a televised presentation could help readers to understand character's attitudes?
A	
B	
C	
20	What are possible factors that can indicate a person's social status?
A	
B	
C	

26. STUDENTS' ACTIVITY #9: **MATCHING THE WORDS TO THE STATEMENTS AND QUESTIONS**

List of words and phrases to choose from:

CODE-SWITCHING	*PROXEMICS*
GRAMMAR	*DIALECT*
LANGUAGE CONTINUUM	*COMMUNICATIVE BEHAVIOURS*
VOCABULARY	*ARTIFACTS*
BASILECT	*THE STANDARD*
PHONOLOGY	*VOCALICS*
FACIAL EXPRESSION	*CHRONEMICS*
ACROLECT	*AUDIENCE*
REGISTERS	*CONTENT*
CREOLE	*CONTEXT*

Match the words from above to these statements or questions.

Where you are saying it? What's the occasion? Who you are saying it to?
What is created when you choose language, content and context?
Mixing of two languages within a situation to discuss particular events.
The set of structural rules governing the composition of clauses, phrases, and words in any given natural language.
In our Creole language this is a continuous spectrum of three varieties that merge into each other.
Words and phrases found in any language.
This variety is the furthest away from the Standard language and considered least prestigious.
The sound system of a language that is concerned with the range of sounds that is possible in a given language.
One example of type of non-verbal communicative behaviour a stern look from your Mum.
This variety of Creole is sometimes confused with the Standard because of it the similarities in grammar and vocabulary.
Has to do with the study of our use of space and how various differences in that use can make us feel more relaxed or anxious.

A form of a language that is spoken in a particular area or community that uses some of its own words, grammar, and pronunciations.
These accompany all our thoughts, words and actions as we try to send a message.
Can be one of the most powerful types of nonverbal communication such as dress, grooming, and jewellery you wear.
The language that is usually the official language used in education and formal situations.
This is not about what you say but how you say it.
Time is the most important factor of this non-verbal communicative behaviour.
A gathering of listeners or spectators; the people addressed by a book, play, film, or a formal interview or meeting.
What you are talking, writing, or reading about.
A language that is born out of the mixture of languages such as English and West African.

27. STUDENTS' ACTIVITY #10: **WORKING WITH A PEER**

To be completed in 20 minutes.

With a partner, discuss each item and then write an example for each of these:

1. An example of **context** where casual register is created.
2. An example of a topic that a person may choose to discuss **using Creole**.
3. An example of a **context in which the Standard** may be considered the **appropriate language** of choice.
4. An **argument** that a **Standard language speaker** would most likely use to **defend** his use of the same language.
5. A list of **4 demographics about an audience** that a speaker should consider.
6. There is a **distinct lack of connection** between the speaker and her audience. What may be responsible for this?
7. '*Standard English is the official language of my country.*' What are **two opposite arguments** when used may evoke this response?
8. How does **history influence** your country's official choice of language?
9. How does **history influence** your country's choice of native dialect?
10. A speaker becomes **very emotional about a memory** of his home country. What language might he lapse into?

28. MODULE TWO ESSAY QUESTIONS FOR PRACTICE

SECTION B
MODULE 2 – LANGUAGE and COMMUNITY

Read the story below carefully and answer the questions that follow.

I looked at my watch. Five minutes to twelve. The situation was bad, but not hopeless. This was not the first time I had found myself without a cent in my pocket and needing to go to the bank urgently. Five minutes before closing time, before that scruffy-faced guard would change the sign to read **CLOSED.**

After that, it would be a trip to paradise or, to be more down-to-earth, lunch with the beautiful Yvette. I needed to make a good impression on this our first date. Hence the flashy tie, the generous splashing of aftershave and Perry Ellis cologne, the dazzling gold imitation wristband. We would sip a glass or two of Dom Perignon, an' I would drool the afternoon away, just gazing into those boldly, big, beautiful, brown eyes.

I made my way through the slow-moving throng of shoppers and idlers on Queen Street, past the loud lottery and incense vendors, past the pirated DVDs and CDs thrust into my face. I skipped down into the street a few times to avoid being crushed to death and maintain the necessary speed. This was going to be close.

It was then, in my side vision that I saw a massive, huge hulking frame making its way towards me. No, I said to myself, O God, not Miss Gladys…not now.

But if it wasn't Miss Gladys, why was the pavement heaving and trembling? Why were stray dogs, vagrants and everyone in her path moving out of the way?

"Poopsie? Poopsie? Is dat you?" said Miss Gladys as she pulled me to her ample bosom.

When the air returned to my lungs after her powerful embrace, I said weakly, *"Robert, Miss Glady,."* as I tried to fix my clothes with trembling hands.

"Yuh forget is I who gih yuh de name 'Poopsie'?" Since one or two passers-by appeared to take mild interest in the proceedings, she found it necessary to add. *"When he was small,l dis boy,"* patting me on my head, *"wuddn't sit down on the potty at all."* I hung my head.

"Buh look how big he get now. Poopsie, how yuh mooma? And yuh brodder? I cud neva remember dat one's name. Is years I didn't see dese chirren… So wha yud doin dese days, boy? Yuh nah workin? When I hear yuh didn't get the scholarship an dey give it to de next boy ah say dey tief yuh. I tell my neighbor dat dey tief yuh. Becuz ever since yuh small it was like yuh was eatin bulbs." All this was said without giving me a chance to respond. Not that I really wanted to anyway.

"Er, excuse me Miss Gladys, I'd love to stand and chat with you but, I am so very sorry but…", straightening and pulling further away from her.

Miss Gladys, looking around at her curious audience, *"I know you want to stand and chat. Yuh did always like chatting. Yuh always wanted to chat down dem girls an dem. Yuh married? Yuh kno my eldest did always like yuh…yuh mus pass and take ah good look at her. She grow up rel nice, nice…yuh remember how thin she was? Well none of dat now…she"*

I pulled back, *"Miss Gladys,"* pleading. *"I must take my leave now. I really must. It's already one minute to twelve"*

Miss Gladys, eyes open wide and pulling back as if I had attacked her, *"What? And is have yuh have me standin here chattin wit yuh? I have to get home to cook for mih husband! Is gone, ah gone yes!"*

With **close referencing of the passage**, discuss in an essay of no more than 500 words:

(a) The dialectal variation used in the passage.
(b) The narrator's reaction and possible justification for his behaviour during his encounter with Ms Gladys
(c) How a video presentation would show the verbal and non-verbal communication between Ms Gladys and the narrator.

Total 25 marks

Read the excerpt below carefully and answer the questions that follow

Living in what many have labelled a hot spot, a high risk community, they knew that they had nothing much going for them. Their mother was both mother and father like so many of their friends. Their father 'bus' and gone so long ago saying that "This life is not for me! I am meant for greatness not living in this stink hole."

The day the CAPE Scholarship came out was the happiest day ever. First to begin Ma get up real early and went to de shop to get de papers early before dem farse neighbours buy dem out! Her words not mine.

I knew when she left the house because I could not sleep. Today was the big day everyone was waiting for. I could not take it any more so I got out of bed and prepared for my mother's return. She wasn't long in returning with the papers folded under her arm.

Before she could sit and open the papers her cell phone rang, steupsing and frowning, she does what has become a habit, she pressed the speakerphone button and answered, *"Mornin' Ms. Elizabet speakin'. How ah cud help yuh?"*

I cringed and waited wondering the identity of the early morning caller.

The voice, "Good morning, is this Ms Elizabeth Johnson?"

"Yea dis is she."

"Is your son Marcus Johnson?"

"Yea dat is mih son."

"Does Marcus attend Belvedere High School and sat CAPE this year, Ma'am?"

"Yea he does atten' dat school. And yea he did sit CAPE. Buh wait ah cud aks yuh why yuh aksing so much question bout mih an mih son?" walking up and down the small room.

"Mother!" trying to get her attention, "It has to do with Scholarship!" I whispered.

"Can I speak to the person, Mother?" reaching for the phone.

"Wha happen boy? Yuh feel ah cyar aks de rite questions? Or better yet talk fancy as you and dat person on de line eh? Yuh feel ah dotish or wha? All ah allyuh is de same. Dem aksing a lot a questions as if ah chupid and you wanting de phone because you feel ah cyar understan de language" all the time talking to me whilst still holding the phone to her ear.

I bowed my head shaking it from side to side. I left the room as in her anger my mother accidentally turned off the phone.

With **close referencing of the passage**, discuss in an essay of no more than 500 words

    (a) The language situation in the excerpt.
    (b) The attitudes to language as revealed in the excerpt.
    (c) The relationship between mother and son.
    (d) How film would effectively capture the communicative behaviours found in this excerpt.

TOTAL 25 marks

Read the excerpt below carefully and answer the questions that follow

Saying goodbye to our Language Arts teacher was for many of us the saddest day in our life. This was a teacher who was our school mother. She was the one teacher whom we knew without a doubt believed in us and wanted the very best for us, her bright shining stars as she always called us.

In her final speech she said to us as we sat there in an unreal silence because we were never silent in Mrs. Joefield's class, she said. *"Young ladies, my bright shining stars, I implore you to continue excelling both in all areas of your life. Be bold, be brave but most of all be disciplined."* Smiling and pointing at me she asked, *"Jassy Marie Reneaud,"* Mrs. Joefield is the only teacher who always call all her students by their full name and surname and we do not feel frightened, *"Do you recall the definition of discipline?"*

Standing I said clearly, *"Discipline is doing what you have to do, whenever you have to do it, even if you do not feel like doing it."*

"Excellent!" Looking at each one of us she said, *"That is what I want each one of you to take with you."*

You can therefore imagine my shock and utter despair when our new Language Arts teacher arrived two days after Mrs. Joefield's departure. Standing with the Principal who came to introduce her to the class, was a not too young female teacher, *"Please sit class! This is Miss Radjay and she is your new Language Arts teacher."*

There was a chorus of *"Good Morning Miss Radjay, welcome to our class!"*

Smiling, our new teacher responded with unaccustomed loudness, *"Yea tanks class. Ah happy to be here too yes!"*

The Principal shook her head and quickly motioned to the teacher to follow her outside. Meanwhile we took the opportunity to quietly whisper about what just took place.

When the door opened a few minutes later, a more subdued Miss Radjay returned sans the Principal. Smiling slightly she said, *"Class I'm so sorry I'd like to apologise for my earlier behaviour. I so accustom talking that way dat I forget that I was talking to you all from a prestige school yes. I do hope that allyuh, sorry you all can forgive me and bear with me.*" looking around the classroom anxiously.

Donna blurted, "*Daz alrite Miss, we cool. Ent girls? We could talk like you when we want and we could speak like Mrs. Joefield when we want also.*"

Sitting and smiling broadly she mimicked, "*Oh goody whenever the Principal is around we will all speak in our best Standard English and den wen we by we self we go code switch and talk we good ole relaxed Creole.*" looking at us for affirmation. There was another chorus of "*Yeh Miss Radjay*"

One of the traitors even went so far to add, "*Miss I rell like dis idea. Sometimes trying to talkin in English whole day is tiring. Dey cyar expect we Creole speakers to forget that dat is we first language you know.*"

I was silent. I could never bring myself to agree to something like that. I could never betray Mrs. Joefield's legacy. And beside how could a teacher Miss Radjay's age speak like that? I could understand if she was a younger person but, she was not and that I could not understand nor forgive her for.

With **close referencing of the passage**, discuss in an essay of no more than 500 words

a) What the difference in language choice of the two teachers reveal about them
b) THREE possible reasons for the reaction of the students to the new teacher
c) What the new teacher hopes to achieve by telling the students "*Oh good den we go code switch whenever de Principal around ent?*"
d) How film would effectively capture communicative behaviours in this excerpt

Total 25 marks

MODULE 2 – LANGUAGE and COMMUNITY

Read the excerpt below carefully and answer the questions that follow

Living in New York had not been easy for Martha. But she struggled and held down three jobs at one time where everyone made her feel like dirt, arriving home just in time to shower in that cold water and hop into her bed. Having done that for seven long years Martha knew when she had had enough. Vowing to get an education and that she did. Now Martha was a teacher and as she stood with her family who came up for her graduation she felt proud of what she had accomplished.

As she said the last sentence of her speech, *"What an exceptional honor it has been to have been chose to address all present. Our academic sojourn has been one of many triumphs and sometimes pain. We have persevered and look at us now. We are graduates ready to embark upon the next phase of our journey. As we do so, we say with one voice…"* As she sat down she did so to a thunderous applause.

Today Martha has come a long way, she was Valedictorian and the promise that she had made to herself so many years ago had been fulfilled. She recalled with dread the early days of attending Touro College in Brooklyn when she was scared stiff to open her mouth.

She recalled the first time the teacher asked her to read a short passage. She took about two minutes before she could even open her mouth to utter the first word. Swallowing slowly she said, *"Readin is important for de society as well as de individual. E--conomics research has establish dat schoolin is an investment dat forms human capital ---dats knowledge…"*

I could still remember the cold dreadful silence that descended on the room. The professor coughed in attempt to cover up her distress. *"Martha, are alright? Can you in future make a serious effort to pronounce and enunciate your words properly?"* Scowling, she called on Miranda who was too eager to take over and show off how well she could read in her proper American Standard language.

I recall the utter shame I felt as I listened to Miranda read. I kept my eyes down in shame and when I took a fleeting peep at the class I saw people looking at Miranda with appreciation. This made me feel even worse. I started to scold myself quietly. *"You had to stand and read in your flat voice? Did you really have to read so stupid in your stupid language? Back home why do you think that that language was not the official language? It for these same reasons and you had to come here and shame yourself? Well, this is the first and last time this will ever happen, the next time I stand to read I will look around and see the same look of appreciation as they had today for Miranda. No one will ever make me feel this way again!"*

With **close referencing of the passage**, discuss in an essay of no more than 500 words

 a) FOUR factors which may have led Martha to choose to get an education.
 b) The language situation present in the extract.
 c) How the communicative behaviours could best be highlighted in a video production of this extract.

Total 25 marks

SECTION B
MODULE 2 – LANGUAGE and COMMUNITY

Read the excerpt below carefully and answer the questions that follow

MISS BENENDICT: Yes, Martha…[*O'Callaghan using the phone in his office, speaks softly.*] So yuh say dat he was questioning you bout me? Buh why? Me an he ent in nothing again. We break up bout ah mont now. Ent ah did tell yuh dat? Me ent want no man who cyar progress wit me and Gerald ent want to progress. Imagine all dat man does want to do is lime wit he friens and dem. An when he done go back home to he mama like ah mamapoole man. I workin now and I intend to move on an up gyurl. I ent dotish or no chupidee. Is money I looking fuh. Him have nutten to offer, mi love … Hol on ah while dey!.

[*She answers another line.*]

Glenn Haven Beach Hotel. Good afternoon Sir. How may I help you? …I'm so sorry, sir, but the Manager, Mr. Joshua Phillip is in a meeting at present. Would you like to speak to the Assistant Manager, Ms Dayna Soogrim? …Very well then Sir. Will you please hold? [Quickly *dials the extension and listens*] I am sorry, sir, but her extension is busy; would you like to hold please or would you like to leave a message?

[*Switching to the next line*]

Hol on ah while dey again, eh Martha gyurl. Ah have to check something.

With **<u>close referencing of the passage</u>**, discuss in an essay of no more than 500 words

  a) FOUR possible factors which may have influenced the writer's choice of languages.
  b) Difficulties that non-West Indians may experience in understanding the excerpt
  c) How the language used reveals the nature of the relationship between Miss Benedict and her callers.
  d) How video would effectively capture the nuances in the excerpt.

Total 25 marks

SECTION B
MODULE 2 – LANGUAGE and COMMUNITY

Read the excerpt below carefully and answer the questions that follow

Maxine: Martha ah want yuh to lissen an lissen good eh. If you want to keep dis job yuh have to understan dis. You see how we does sit down and talk roun in de back here? You cyar do dat in di front. You understan?

Martha: Yes, Ma'am.

Maxine: Gyur you an me is friens, so when we in di back here doh bodder to call me Ma'am gyurl! So as ah was sayin when we workin roun' di front is different business. Is plenty different people does come to stay here you kno an so you does have to kno which accent to use wit each one ah dem! You understan me?

Martha: [Shaking head vigorously] Yes ah understan. Even doh ah doh kno why we have to speak like dem odder people an not speak in we own language. But doh worry wit me you kno I is ah Boss when it come to talkin to touris an dem.

Maxine: Ok well leh we try you out now! So I is a 'Merican jus come in an ah say "Oh hiii Arrhhhmmm looking for the loo. Carrrrrn you direct me to it?" Tell mih wha yuh go tell she?

Martha: Daz rell easy gyrul I go put on mih bestest accent an ah go say, "Ma'rrrrm sure arrhh carrrn direct you tuh the loo. Arrrmmm, will yuh please, arrrhhh follow me, Ma'rrrrm?" So how ah do?

Maxine: Bloody, jolly good! [Slapping Martha on the shoulder] Bloody, jolly good my deeaah! [The both double over with laughter] Do you kno which language ah jus talk dey?

Martha: Swear language? All dem bloody dis and bloody dat is swear words to mi. Ah hope yuh doh expec a proper church gyurl as me to swear like dat?

Maxine: Look jus' play it by ear. Jus play it by ear!

With **close referencing of the passage**, discuss in an essay of no more than 500 words

(a) The assumption which Maxine makes about the appropriateness of Creole language.

(b) Whether their choice of American is motivated by linguistic or non-linguistic factors.

(c) What Maxine's advice reveals about her attitudes to members of her community and to visitors.

(d) '... *ah doh kno why we have to speak like dem odder people an not speak in we own language'.*
How would you respond to this concern of Martha?

(e) FOUR ways in which a televised presentation of this situation would enhance the comedic effect of this passage

Total 25 marks

SECTION B
MODULE 2 – LANGUAGE and COMMUNITY

Read the poem below carefully and answer the questions that follow.

Robbie yuh goin in de market wid mih in de mornin rite?
Do I really have to, Mother dear?
Yes yuh have to boun to and must to!
Since yuh come back home all yuh doin is sittin in front ah dat damn computer
Talkin to dem foreign friens ah yours
Yuh home now
Yuh have to behave as if yuh home
So yuh coming wit min in de mornin!
Take a lil res from de internet
From yapping yapping on Skype
Ah fed up hearin dem foreign language
"Oh hiiiiii Robbie, Rob, Bob…"
"How are you Robbie, Rob, Bob…?"
"How's the weatherrrr Robbie, Rob, Bob?"
Yuh home now so get on so!

"Allyuh come an get yuh sweet orange, plenty sweet orange!"
Buh aye aye Mistress Jackson is dat little Robert?"
Buh look how nice an big he get?
He is ah doctor already?"
Yeah Singh man! Yeah he is big doctor now!
And if yuh hear he Singh yuh eh go understan de boi you kno.
Robbie talk to Sigh nah boi
You an Singh uses to talk plenty when you was small
"Motherrr ahhh you are putting me in a precariously embarrassing position."
Yuh see wha ah tellin yuh Singh boi?
Robbie wha you feel like eatin today Sunday?
Ah nice stew pork?
No Mother ahhm not eatin meat. Remember I'm a pescatarian now."
Yuh are what? Ah Pisces but yuh is a Libran born in October!
No mother I am a pescatarian, I abstain from all meats with the exception of fish!

Boi I Singh livin so long an I never hear dat word in mih life.

Boi talk in we language when yuh wit we nah man.

Yuh could use dem high fullutten language when yuh wit yuh foreign friens yuh modder tell me bout. Rite? Talk we talk when yuh wit we! Okay?

Dat is true cause watever you are... it soun rell dotish to me.

Foreign make you chupid instead ah smart when it comes to eatin food. Ent Singh boi

Dat is why yuh so skinny. Yuh need some ah mih pork and stew chicken

Better yet yuh need ah good pepper pot wit all dem meat together!

"Motherrrrr you are making my stomach churrrrn! Urghhhh"

Mr. Singh what are these poor animals tied up here?

So boi yuh tellin me yuh doh recognise dem tings?

One time yuh even uses to go and help mih ketch dem same tings. Hah

Well touch dem an you go remember

Go ahead touch dem! Ah bet you go remember!

Oh Gad! Oh Gad! Somebody take dis blasted crab from of mih han, please!

Oh Gad! Oh Gad!

Come lemme help yuh.

Yuh see ent yuh remember?

Edlin Rochford
2015

In an ESSAY of no more than 500 words, discuss the following:

a) What Robert hopes to achieve by using the Standard English in this situation
b) What factors may have led to the varying reactions of the narrator and Singh in the poem to Robbie's language choice
c) How a video presentation of this scene would highlight the varying reactions to Robbie's behaviour.

Total 25 marks

Read the poem below carefully and answer the questions that follow

Ah Shame

Aye gyul ah glad to see yuh come back home
But gyurl whey de white fella yuh had?
Wat yuh an he done! Yuh cyar take on he!
Steups gyurl how yuh dotish so?
I was so glad when yuh did come home las year wit yuh white man
I was so glad to see how he treatin yuh like a lady
I was so glad it wasn't ah damn ragga ragga like dat good fuh nutten Vibot
Mother the boy's name is not Vibot its Virbert, mother!
There is an "r" in his name so please use it!
Wat everrrr he still is ah witless good fuh nutten!
So whey is Roberrrrt? Mih white son in law?
Boiii ah did like to hear him speak
And did like to hear him call mih name 'Marrrtheerrr"
Urrrrr it made me feel like somebody
Not like when dat no good nutten wutless
Vibot spoil mih name wit he "Mata" dis and 'Mata" dat
Steups man ah does want to hit he in he mout
Gyurl when yuh live in 'Merica fuh soooo long
Yuh have a rite to come back better dan yuh leave dis place
Yuh shoudda come back talkin better,
Yuh shudda come back lookin better
So whey yuh white man? Mih future son in law?
Is he who wouda help yuh to talk, look and be better
Yu eh see Myra when she come back afta six monts
Dat gyurl change so good
Ah mean she language sounded nice
Wit ah nice 'Merican lickle accent
An yuh remember John who work only
One week wid de Merican couple

He talk so nice now
Gyurl, yuh couldn improve yuhself?
Everybody go come lookin and expectin jus dat
Wha gyurl do talk chupidness! Is joke yuh makin rite?
Yuh wah kill yuh modder here? Is wha yuh sayin?
Yuh come back home to marry who? Vibot?
Look ah go say it how de hell ah want- Vibot! Vibot! Vibot!
An dat is how ah go always call he Vibot!
Ah shame!

Edlin D. Rochford
2015

With **<u>close referencing of the passage</u>**, discuss in an essay of no more than 500 words

a) What the narrator's behaviour reveals about her attitude to the use of Creole and American English.
b) What THREE possible factors may have influenced Myra and John's attitude and choice of dialectal variety
c) How the narrator's shame could be highlighted in a video presentation of this scene.

Total 25 marks

SECTION B
MODULE 2 – LANGUAGE and COMMUNITY

Read the excerpt below carefully and answer the questions that follow

As I sat there I felt the familiar coldness encasing my stomach region creeping, creeping upwards to finally encircle my heart. There is nothing here for me the voice inside whispered. This land, these people and this culture is foreign to me and I longed for to be home. In the warmth on a beach listening to familiar sing song lilting nuances of my language. There was nothing I knew, nothing to comfort me.

I listened. The group in their usual huddle was speaking softly but yet not softly. They didn't want me to hear and yet they did. The informal group leader Shantelle was talking softly. Melissa was crying as she always seems to be these days. All of a sudden someone began singing. I tried to make out the singer but it was difficult because of their positioning, so I tried to make out the words. *"Ma belle, ma belle, maaaa belle ka di".* I really don't know why I even bothered to listen because whatever they are singing or saying was dangerous. They were 'bad talking me' and I know it.

I must protect myself. I began leaving the room softly but even if I had not the group would not have stopped what they are doing. I could see Melly, their pet name for her, being comforted. Even when she threatened me to throw the chair at me, she did so with a kind of *'fakeness'.* As I got to the door I heard someone say, *"Ti moun,"* and another voice saying, *"Doudou che,"* while twirling the head of the pencil that was wrapped around a pencil. *"Do do l'enfant do."* As I closed the door and hurried away all of a sudden I began to feel light headed, sleepy and cold.

With **close referencing of the passage**, discuss in an essay of no more than 500 words

  (a) THREE possible factors which may have motivated Shantelle to lapse into French Creole to comfort Melissa.
  (b) The narrator's attitudes to what she is overhearing
  (c) How far the narrator's feelings of alienation may be influenced by her inability to understand the language that the group is speaking
  (d) FOUR ways in which a video presentation of this scene would highlight the narrator's feelings of unease.

Total 25 marks

SECTION C

29.   THE FORMAT OF MODULE THREE ESSAY QUESTION IN PAPER 02

In Module 3 essay you are asked to read a short scenario and respond to the instructions. The instructions may look like these below:

In an essay of no more than 500 words

a) Identify an appropriate channel or medium you would effectively promote the campaign
b) Compose your message or your feature address
c) Targeting of THREE different kinds of audience in the campaign
d) Evaluation of the campaign

Total 25 marks

In this Module Three essay you are expected to include what you have learned from Module One and Module Two essays. For example in this essay you may use as many of these as possible:

Organizational strategies such as

> ➢ referencing reputable institutions
> ➢ experts opinion
> ➢ statistical data
> ➢ cause and effect

30. POSSIBLE GENRES IN MODULE THREE ESSAY:

- Proposal
- Feature address or speech
- Advertisement
- Formal letter
- A campaign

31. THE ACTIONS YOU MAY BE ASKED TO PERFORM IN MODULE THREE ESSAYS:

- Discuss the **approach**...
- Write a **proposal**...
- Write a **feature address** or **speech**...
- In **an essay** discuss how you propose to...
- Write a **formal letter**...
- Compose your **presentation**...

32. HOW TO WRITE OR COMPOSE A FEATURE ADDRESS OR SPEECH:

- Introduce yourself to the audience and state very briefly why you are there? What gives you the right to be there? What is the topic of your address?

- If there are words or terms in your address then you may need to define these terms?
- Give examples of what you are saying.
- Use the **PEE** format (**P**- make your point, **E**- give an example and **E**- give an explanation)

33. HOW TO WRITE AN ESSAY

- Your introduction (a summary of what's in the scenario and the statements)
- Your body/containing the answers to the statements for the scenario
- You may **justify** or give **reasons** for whatever you decide to do
- A conclusion

34. HOW TO COMPOSE A PRESENTATION

- Write whatever it is as if you are speaking directly to the audience
- Do not ever justify or give reasons here
- You indicate this by using a direct greeting and Personal Pronouns (I, You, we, our, your)
- In a presentation you may end with a summary or a conclusion

35. THE FEATURES OF A PROPOSAL

- Your introduction is like the essay's
- Your body is composed of words like 'propose' or 'intend' or 'going to' or 'would do'
- You must justify whatever you say you intend to do

36. HOW TO COMPOSE AN ADVERTISEMENT

Firstly:

- The language of advertisement is Persuasive
- Advertisers aim to reach people on three levels
    - The **Logos** so they appeal logically with reasons
    - The **Pathos** so they appeal to your emotions
    - The **Ethos** so they appeal to your sense of credibility

Secondly:

There are various types of advertisements techniques that you can use as examples:

- **Bandwagon** type (*everybody doing it and if you are not you are missing out*)
- **Brand Appeal** type (*Everybody's wearing Nike! The world loves Levi Jeans!*)
- **Celebrity type** (*Jah Cure/Machel Montano/Ravi B/Destra Garcia/ TallPree to advertise product*)

NB: There are many more types of advertisement techniques.

37. THE DIFFERENT MEDIA THAT ARE USED IN CAMPAIGN

- Online media, including interactive ads and banners on websites
- Print media includes newspapers, magazines, and print directories
- Social media /Digital media include internet advertising, webcasts, web pages, mobile and text ads, interactive media, including social media networks
- Direct mail using the postal service or couriers
- Email
- Radio Broadcast media: Includes TV and radio
- Television Broadcast media: Includes TV and radio
- Telemarketing
- Events and trade shows
- Search engines
- Outdoor media includes billboards, transit signs, murals, and signage.

38. POSSIBLE FACTORS TO CONSIDER WHEN DOING MODULE THREE ESSAY

- The audience
- The language you are going to use
- The register that is created
- The strategies that you will use to reach your target audience

- The medium or channel
- The evaluation strategies that you will use

39. MARKING SCHEME WITH ALLOCATION OF MARKS FOR MODULE THREE ESSAY

Content	10
A superior response that addresses **all areas** identified	**9-10**
A good response that addresses **most of the areas** identified	**7-8**
A fair response that addresses **half of the areas identified**; however, not all fully developed	**5-6**
A weak response — **less than half of** expected content Not well developed	**3-4**
A **poor response.** Minimal content evident	**0-2**

Organization (5 for body + 2 for formal features)	7
Excellent introduction, thematic cohesion, appropriate use of transitional devices, effective conclusion. (Include consideration of formal structure of letter)	7
Good use of the above with one to two weaknesses visible	**5-6**
Adequate level of organization with several weaknesses noted	**3-4**
Unsatisfactory level of organization. Weakness in all areas identified above	**1-2**

Expression	8
Excellent, effective and error free use of language	8
Very good use of language though there may be a few lapses	7
Good use of language though there may be a few lapses	**5-6**
Some ability to use language accurately and effectively, but with some inconsistency in accurate usage	**3-4**
Frequent, inaccurate use of language OR Insufficient information presented	**1-2**
Inability to use language accurately OR Too little information presented to make an assessment	**0**

40. STUDENTS' ACTIVITY #11: **FILL IN THE BLANKS IN EACH PASSAGE USING THE WORDS AND PHRASES IN THE BOXES BELOW.**

A. All communication begins with _____ and ends with _____. There needs to be a _____ for the message to be successfully conveyed, but that does not guarantee _____. The sender is responsible for_____, but that does not mean that he or she has absolute control over _____ Clarity of _____ is obviously important, but not always easy to know beforehand. The sender's personality, beliefs, cultural, education all _____ and it is important for the sender to be aware of this as he or she is _____ the message. Simply put, _____ is translating information into _____ that represent the ideas or concepts of the message that needs sending. These symbols are usually words in _____form. To ensure _____, the sender should know as much about his or her _____ as possible in order to focus and support the encoding process.

successful communication	Symbols	written or spoken
Success	encoding	the process
influences the message	Message	the receiver
Encoding	Receiver	successful conveyance
the sender	audience or the receiver	

B. In addition to this awareness of self and encoding, the sender must choose the proper channel to _____ .Using the wrong channel may result in _____. A _____ can take many forms and can change depending upon the type of message being sent and the desired_____. If one of those desired outcomes is _____, a hand-written _____would probably not be the best choice. Written and oral channels can take on a variety of forms. _____, email and texting are everywhere today; however, _____ need to be considered. There are times when _____ is not appropriate or when a face-to-face communication is preferred over a phone call.

Channel	outcomes of the message	miscommunication
social protocols	convey the message	Telephones and computers
postal-delivered letter	an email or a text	immediate feedback

C. Like senders, _____ are influenced by internal factors: _____, their receptivity to _____ or their relationship to the sender, their _____, mood, or state of mind can affect a message. Their _____ culture and prior knowledge can also alter _____ reception.

their personality	current feelings	the message
Education	Receivers	successful message

D. Once the message moves through the _____, the receiver _____ it. The _____ then _____ the sent symbols and attempts to assign some _____ to them and to the message in general. The receiver uses his or her own _____ and the _____ of the message to _____ its meaning.

receiver	interpret	interprets	Decodes
experience	channel	meaning	Context

E. _____ is the return message from receiver to sender; a _____ to the message that can take any number of forms. Even a _____ can be interpreted as feedback. It is the _____ that enables the sender to know whether the message was received _____ or not. Therefore it is essential to the _____.

Response	Feedback	non-response
communication process	Feedback	successfully

F. This _____, though very common, is _____ with potential _____ at every turn. Spoken or language is inherently easy to _____. Even a certain look or facial expression can be misinterpreted and cause _____. A misplaced comma or a thoughtful pause in response to a _____ can be mistaken for another _____. All of these possibilities (and many more!) are considered _____, which is anything that can interfere with any part of the _____. Noise can be literally _____ that comes from some outside source. It can also come _____ from a sender or receiver's thoughts or. _____

is when the sent message was successfully received and the _____ provides the sender with desirable _____ .

physical noise	feedback	noise	Intention
misinterpret	process	receiver	Internally
communication process	Effective Communication	breakdown and barriers	breakdowns
written	fraught	question	Perceptions

41. SOME SUGGESTIONS FOR RESPONSES TO MODULE THREE ESSAY DISCUSSION TOPICS IN CAPE PAST PAPERS

Discussion topic – Indicate an appropriate channel or medium that you would use to inform villagers of a deadly disease threat

- The audience and its demographics (age, occupation education level and geographic location) always influence the use of any channel or medium.
- The cost that is attached to using a medium, the speed at which you want the message transmitted, whether the receivers or audience (villagers) influence the choice of medium.
- The scope of the medium to reach all of the villagers to ensure that they all get the message influences the choice of medium.
- In this situation the audience consists of members of a village community. Being a village one can believe that the location may not warrant the use of too much technology: (even though this may seem stereotypical, it's is a pertinent reality)
- Possible channel can be a community meeting in the community centre and where at the end you hand out a simple handout with a summarised version of the message or travelling around in a vehicle using a PA(Public Address) system with a pre-recorded message or making house to house visits.
- **"Composing your presentation"** – Write what you will present to the villagers as if you are standing in front of them and speaking about the disease. For example you will

introduce yourself, say why you are there, what qualifies you to be there etc. Then you will identify the name of the disease, how the disease is spread, what are the particular symptoms, what must be done to curb the spread of the disease, and what to do if any villager should contract the disease.

Discussion topic – Write a paragraph explaining the appropriateness of your composition.

- In this paragraph you are to justify or give reason as to your choice of language in your presentation, the information you presented and the channel you used etc

Discussion topic - The communication challenges you would expect to find when targeting the vendors.

- Communication challenges in terms of language i.e. should I use Creole or Standard English? The vocabulary I use should be simple enough to be understood but not to come across to the audience as condescending.
- The possibility exists that many, if not all of the vendors may not have gained a high level of education and so you should take this into consideration.
- The fact that getting persons to do things differently especially if they are accustomed to doing things the same way for all their lives

Discussion topic - The information that must be relayed and the vocabulary and register you would consider appropriate

- The information that must be relayed is relevant to the topic at hand. Your vocabulary and chosen language are influenced by the audience and all its demographics. Likewise your register is created by the language that you have chosen and the context where the situation is taking place. For example if you chose Creole language it will be because the audience speaks and understands this language or the audience is your friend or family or the context is appropriate. Creole as the choice language creates a casual or informal or intimate or consultative register.
- Use simple everyday structures as far as possible
- Try as far as possible to make minimal use of jargons and technical words and phrases
- Use narrative and conversational tone

Discussion topic – Write a feature address in which specific motivational terms are emphasised e.g. a speech to students of 'peace and love' **or** 'respect, tolerance and togetherness'

- In a situation like this you can begin your address the usual way with a brief introduction about yourself, why you are there and what qualifies you to being there. After this you can define each term and give an example of the term and an example of what is not.

Discussion topic – The medium for presenting an advertisement

- **Direct mail** has the highest impact of any medium. Your message reaches each recipient in a personalized way and at a moment they have chosen to consider your message. The cost of reaching an individual through direct mail can be even greater than television, making it the most expensive advertising medium per person reached.
- **Television** also offers the advertiser an opportunity to speak to a captive audience. In fact, television viewers are even more apt to fully "tune into" an advertisement. The cost, though, of purchasing a television spot is even greater than that of radio.
- **Radio** offers a dramatic improvement over "print" advertisements. The "listener" is captive to the message unless they switch stations or turn the radio off. The cost to reach the same amount of people that a print ad would reach, however, is significantly higher.
- **Outdoor and transit** advertisements such as billboards, transit signs, murals, and signage are hard to avoid viewing. But, despite the high visibility factor, no one spends any great amount of time reading them. They are appropriate for very simple messages.
- **Magazines** offer a slightly better opportunity to catch the reader's attention. Readers tend to peruse magazines more carefully than they do newspapers, and because magazine ads are placed fewer per page, the competition for the reader's eye is reduced. But magazine ads cost more than newspaper ads.
- **Yellow Pages** can be a wonderful venue, and even the best choice, for a few business-to-business companies in the service sector, but is totally inappropriate for most others especially product-based businesses.
- **Newspapers** are generally the cheapest way to reach a mass audience. However, newspapers carry many ads. It is easy for all but the largest display ads to get lost in the visual clutter. In any case, remember that newspapers are typically browsed by the reader. If an ad is seen at all, the headline will be glimpsed and the copy largely ignored.

Discussion topic – Describe those strategies and visual aids that could be used to enhance your presentation to both audiences

- Posters
  Charts
  PowerPoint slides
  Models
  Pictures/photos
  Dry erase boards
  Overhead transparencies
  Puppet show
  Movie clips
  Audio clips

Discussion topic – Your proposal must address the <u>maintenance of the theme</u> **of a campaign**

- You can maintain your theme through the use of a variety of media such as speeches, discussion, dramatic presentations, songs, jingles, T-shirts
- You can use different channels such as TV, radio, Facebook, theatre, newspapers, bumper stickers
- Maintenance of the theme is dependent on the effort that you put into the daily bombardment over the specific period of time.

Discussion topic – Your proposal must address targeting difference kinds of audience in the campaign

- The members of the community are the various audiences which you need to put into categories according to age, gender, education, occupation, ethnicity etc
- Choose a medium that will best deliver the message to each of the audiences

Discussion topic – Evaluation of the campaign

- You must still decide which evaluation method(s) to use. For example, if you are interested in knowing whether a community campaign was successful in influencing how community members view their relationship with the environment, you may select attitudes toward recycling as the indicator of change. But how can you measure attitudes toward the environment? Could you use a questionnaire? Might personal interviews be appropriate?

What other methods could you use to evaluate?

Focus groups

Suggestion box

Face book page

Observation

Discussion topic – The appeals to the target group

- Whenever you are asked to discuss 'appeals' you are to remember that a seller, a debater or anyone who is trying to win or persuade someone always appeal on grounds of ethos, pathos and logos and so they:
- Appeal to reason or logic, using facts and figures
- Appeal to emotions, using emotive words and slogans; jingles; visuals;
- Appeal to ethos

Discussion topic – The effectiveness of strategies to be used to encourage awareness

- Use of catchy tune or jingle
- Use of popular local personality as voice over
- Placing ads in school newspapers or magazine pull-out
- Sponsoring school-related or community based events
- Use of promotional merchandise like cups, key rings with the name of company, pencils, pencil cases, pens, knapsacks, tote bags, T-shirts, wrist band
- Creation of a mascot that will appear at malls

Discussion topic – Justification for at least THREE specific strategies to be used to promote a campaign in a school community

- Posters to attract and inform
- Banners to attract, inform and excite
- Articles in school newspaper – aimed at informing and winning credibility
- Messages posted on social network sites/media – to attract the extended school community (Facebook, Instagram, blog, Google+)

- Face –to- face invitation – adding that personalized touch to the campaign
- T – Shirts to advertise the campaign
- Use of different varieties of language - to appeal to different kinds of audiences
- Use of different registers – to appeal to different kinds of audiences

42. MODULE THREE ESSAY QUESTIONS FOR PRACTICE

SECTION C
MODULE 3 – SPEAKING and WRITING

The advertisement below is an example of advertisements found in any form of communication. Imagine that you are a member of a community consumer awareness group, which informs individuals of the negatives of advertising. Indicate an appropriate medium, which your group would use to convince an audience of young persons of the dangers inherent in advertisements. Compose your presentation.

[25 marks]

DON'T BE LEFT OUT!
DON'T BE LEFT BEHIND!
BE PART OF THE GANG!
DRINK SWING.
SWING IS 'DE BES' DRINK OF THE YOUNG CROWD.
SWING KEEPS YOU HAPPY, ENERGETIC AND POPULAR.

Swing

DRINK
AND YOU WON'T BE LEFT BEHIND!

SECTION C
MODULE 3 – SPEAKING and WRITING

Read the scenario below and answer the questions that follow.

You have been asked by the Health Ministry in your country to lead a team of workers in a health campaign in a rural village where there have been several reported cases of the deadly Dengue Haemorrhagic Virus. You and your team are required to advise the community of the dangers of this disease and also to recommend precautions which should be put in place.

In an ESSAY of no more than 300 words:

(a) Identify in a paragraph an appropriate medium that you and your team would use to create such awareness of this deadly disease in the village.

(b) Compose your presentation paying close attention to language use, vocabulary, register and organizational strategies.

(c) Write a paragraph explaining the appropriateness of your presentation.

Total 25 marks

SECTION C
MODULE 3 – SPEAKING and WRITING

Read the scenario below and answer the questions that follow.

The Community Center in your area has for years been plagued by a rat infestation. As a member of the Youth group that uses the space you have advocated to the relevant authority to have something done. Finally, the problem was rectified and in an effort to keep the space clean, you were asked to conduct a series of meetings to make those who use the Center aware of their responsibilities. You are quite aware that cleanliness is a sensitive matter and must be handled as such.

In an ESSAY of no more than 500 words discuss how you propose to make this project an effective one in terms of:

(a) Maintenance of the theme of the project.
(b) Targeting the various users of the Center.
(c) The language and register (s).
(d) Evaluation of the project.

Total 25 marks

Read the scenario below and answer the questions that follow.

The Mayor of the Capital City has called for the ban on glass bottles at all public events in the city for the Carnival season. You have been asked to be the youth representative in a committee with the responsibility of planning and executing a campaign that would sensitize all stakeholders on the issue.

Discuss your approach in terms of:

(a) Three strategies that you and the committee would use in the campaign to sensitize the people and the justification for each of these strategies.
(b) Language registers and varieties that would be considered appropriate.
(c) The information you think must be relayed during the campaign.
(d) Three strategies that could be used to evaluate the campaign.

Total 25 marks

SECTION C
MODULE 3 – SPEAKING and WRITING

Read the scenario below and answer the questions that follow.

As the youngest member of a popular advertising firm, you were surprised you were asked to design an advertisement promoting the theme of the benefits of organic foods over fast foods. The target audience is a mixture of pre-teens and teenagers who are generally known to have a preference for fast foods. You were offered a cash incentive upon successful completion of the proposal for the advertisement and presentation of it to the Board of Directors.

In an ESSAY of no more than 500 words write your PROPOSAL for the advertisement that you will present to the Board of Directors. Your proposal must consider the following:

    (a) The information about four benefits of named organic foods.
    (b) Appropriate languages and registers you would consider.
    (c) What strategies you would use in making a visual presentation of the advertisement.
    (d) The medium you would consider effective for presenting the advertisement to the Board.

Total 25 marks

SECTION C
MODULE 3 – SPEAKING and WRITING

Read the scenario below and answer the questions that follow.

You are the School counsellor at Abercromby High School in your country. You have been approached by the President of the school's Peer Counselling club seeking your professional help on the topic of bullying amongst the students. Because of the sensitive nature of the topic parents were invited to attend as well. In a proposal to the Principal and the President do the following:

(a) Identify and justify the difference in the approach that would be used in the address to BOTH audiences. Your proposal should focus on the content, language and register.
(b) THREE strategies that would be effective in encouraging awareness in the audiences.
(c) Identify those visual aids that could also be used to enhance your presentation.

Total 25 marks

SECTION C
MODULE 3 – SPEAKING and WRITING

Read the scenario below and answer the questions that follow.

As a Dean, your concerns have led you to investigate the negative effects of social media on secondary school teenagers. You decided to hold a seminar to create awareness about the effects of prolong use of social media. The seminar will be delivered to the school's population.

(a) In no more than 60 words, explain how you would use TWO visual aids, to enhance your delivery.

(b) In no more than 300 words, write the feature address which you would deliver at the upcoming seminar.

(c) In your address, discuss THREE effects of social media on the school population.

Total 25 marks

SECTION C
MODULE 3 – SPEAKING and WRITING

Read the scenario below and answer the questions that follow.

Your community is located in an area where enthusiasts come annually to '***turtle watch***' the Leatherbacks. You are a member of an environment protection group that is concerned about the actions of the visitors towards the turtles and the environment. The stakeholders are being persuaded to join in a planned protest march where the intention is to sensitize all stakeholders to the potential threat and possible solutions.

(a) Indicate an appropriate medium that your group would use to effectively achieve your purpose.

(b) Compose your presentation

(c) Write a paragraph explaining the appropriateness of your composition.

Total 25 marks

Read the scenario below and answer the questions that follow.

"Volunteers are the lifeblood of the Olympic Games and part of the DNA of thousands of people in this country," said Sebastian Coe, Chair of the London 2012 Organising Committee, when the volunteer programme was launched.

Your country has been selected to host the regional Under -20 Football Tournament. Interested persons are invited to volunteer to serve in the capacity of events volunteers, safety team members and medical support.

As one of the volunteer coordinators, you are mandated to organize a campaign to persuade volunteers to fill these THREE positions.

In an ESSAY format, write a PROPOSAL to present to the organizers. In your proposal you should provide details and examples on:

(a) Strategies that you would use to persuade EACH target group.
(b) Register to be used with EACH of the THREE target groups.
(c) The media to be used to persuade EACH group to volunteer.

Total 25 marks

SECTION C
MODULE 3 – SPEAKING and WRITING

Read the scenario below and answer the questions that follow.

The Peer Counselling group at your school has decided to organize a campaign to promote anti-bullying among the school community. As a member of the group you have been asked to develop a proposal for presentation to the school's administration.

In an essay of no more than 500 words, present

(i) Your proposal, including such items as the theme, timetable of events, personnel who will be involved and the benefits to the school

(ii) Justification for at least THREE specific strategies to be sued in the promoting of this campaign

Total 25 marks

43. STUDENTS' ACTIVITY #12: **THE FUNCTIONS OF NON-VERBAL COMMUNICATION**

Read the scenarios and choose the correct function from the list below each scenario.

The amount of redundancy nonverbal communication adds to the verbal message for example if you say *"Hi"* or *"Bye"* you will probably wave your hand also, and if you say you're hungry you might rub your stomach. If something tastes bad you would express your dislike accompanied with a disgusted look on your face. The function of the non-verbal here is?

Contradiction, Regulation, Accentuation, Substitution, Reinforcement

Whenever you use a nonverbal action or cue instead of speaking, for example instead of actually saying *"hi"* or *"bye"* you might just wave a hand at someone. When you are not able to speak to a person you use a nonverbal cue. The function of the non-verbal here is?

Contradiction, Regulation, Accentuation, Substitution, Reinforcement

When you use a nonverbal message to negate the verbal message; for example if you ask how someone is and they say "good" but they roll their eyes or look down at the floor and shrug their shoulders, you know they are actually not good and they have just negated the verbal message they were sending. The function of the non-verbal here is?

Contradiction, Regulation, Accentuation, Substitution, Reinforcement

When you use of nonverbal cues to intensify the verbal message; for example if you speak louder and quickly you are adding intensity to the verbal message. We can tell when a person is excited because they usually speak loud and their eyes widen, making the message clearer. The function of the non-verbal here is?

Contradiction, Regulation, Accentuation, Substitution, Reinforcement

In a conversation when persons take turns for conversational order; for example persons may use hand signals to indicate that they are done talking and it is someone else's turn to talk. The function of the non-verbal here is?

Contradiction, Regulation, Accentuation, Substitution, Reinforcement

44.   STUDENTS' ACTIVITY #13: **UNDERSTANDING NON-VERBAL COMMUNICATION**

Nonverbal communication is the use of gestures, facial expressions, and other non-audible expressions to transmit a message.

	Gestures, facial expressions, and other non-audible expressions
1	Maintaining eye contact is a sign of … … … … … … ….
2.	Avoiding eye contact is clearly indicative … … … … … ..
3.	A soft smile is a sign of … … .
4.	A rigid smile or a smirk may be a sign of … …
5.	Raised eyebrows are not only a sign of surprise; but may be … … …
6.	Frowning is facial expression that we tend to assume… … …
7.	Frowning also gives out the message that we are ….
8.	Standing erect shows confidence, …
9.	Constant fiddling with everything in sight is a sign of … …
10.	Standing with your hands crossed behind you, combined with your facial expressions … … .
11.	If you are angry, you may be ….
12.	You may be constantly shaking your legs … … ….
13.	Pointing to oneself is a sign of ….
14.	Rubbing your hands together … ..
15.	If you are sitting perfectly still but are leaning backwards … … ….

Use these words and phrases to complete the statements in the boxes above

	Words and phrases
A	… … contempt.
B	… … anxiety, frustration, boredom, and lack of interest.
C	… ….as a sign of your nervousness or fear of confrontation.
D	….....a natural physical trait of some people, and they may do it without realizing
E	… ….when under stress.
F	… ….but if you are slouching, it is a sign of low self-esteem.
G	… … indicates excitement and readiness to engage in an activity.
H	… ….confidence and positivity.
I	… ….may be a clear sign of anger or frustration that you are trying to hold back.

J	… ….this gives the impression of disinterest or even downright disagreement.
K	… ….unapproachable and cold.
L	… … discomfort and lack of confidence.
M	… … encouragement.
N	… ….clenching your fists.
O	… ….denial.

45. POSSIBLE ANSWERS FOR MODULE ONE PAST PAPER ESSAY QUESTIONS IN PAPER 02

Possible Language Techniques and Organizational Strategies in Module One of Paper O2 Past Papers

2003

- Rhetorical questions
- Hyperboles or exaggerations
- Reference to notable achievement
- Allusions to historical data
- Compare and contrast
- Emotive words

2003

- Personifications
- Repetitions
- Comparison and contrast
- Metaphors
- Similes
- Alliterations
- References to historical data
- Visual imagery

2004

- Short paragraphing
- Rhetorical questions
- Problem solution

- Referencing to past surveys
- Comparison and contrast
- Referencing of experts or authority
- Hyperboles
- Statistical data
- Examples

2005

- Personification
- Historical data and artefacts
- Pun/coinage of words
- Humour
- Conversational tone
- Appeal to audience through personal pronouns
- Appeal to authority to add credibility
- Use of punctuation (dash, hyphen, exclamation, ellipsis) so to enhance the conversational tone of the excerpt
- Compare/contrast of local expert opinion with that of the more established historians to add validity

2006

- Rhetorical questions which adds to the contrast of the piece
- Presentation of the problems that affect both genders
- Emotive language which highlight felt frustration and distress
- Use of anecdotes which add authenticity to the piece
- Contrasts
- Reporting of personal experiences
- Use of 2nd person pronouns to add intimacy
- Tone of frustration or concern
- Tone of contempt

2007

- Compare and contrast
- Directly addressing the audience
- Use of first –person narrative
- Use of Creole and Standard

- Anecdotal responses or examples
- Use of rhetorical questions
- Factual data report from a website
- Referencing of expert advice
- Information from a creditable source or authority
- Tongue –in-cheek hopeful comment
- Clear change of the tone of the piece
- Movement from specific to general

2008 (1st and 2nd)

- Use of humour
- Narrative discourse
- Dialogue/introspection and narrative discourse
- Analogy
- Contrast
- Juxtaposition of thought
- Intensive reporting of characters' thoughts
- Contractions
- Exclamations
- Repetition of simple short sentences
- Dramatic opening phrase
- Repeated allusion
- Document put forward by respected academics
- Referencing of newspapers and international news
- Emotive words
- Exclamation marks
- Reference to official report
- Language that create unease

2009

- Referencing of reputable institution or organization
- Presentation of differing ways illiteracy is manifested
- Examples of effects of illiteracy
- Benefits
- Contrast

- Repetition
- Use of academic language

2010

- Use of factual data
- Use of statistical data
- Comparison and contrast
- Different categories of stories
- Use of cue words
- Step by step process approach
- Rhetorical questions
- Serious and critical tone
- Metaphor
- Opinion of specialist and expert

2011

- Use of analogy
- Detailed information
- Historical record
- Scientific data
- Comparison
- Details or examples of destructive power
- Chronological sequencing
- Causes and effects
- Emotive words
- Visual and auditory imagery
- Narrative prose
- Comparison and contrast
- Use of auditory and visual metaphor

2012

- Definition
- Comparison
- Technical details
- Information presented in sequential order
- Expert advice

- Logical presentation of strengths and weaknesses
- Short paragraphs
- Contrast of ideas

2013

- Opinion of a reliable source of information
- Contrasting reasons
- Use of cause and effect
- Use of illustrations/examples
- Urging UWI to consider other initiatives to benefit the consumer
- Concluding with a stimulating idea
- Use of relatively short paragraphs to facilitate processing of the argument
- Use of short paragraphs to isolate specific points
- Clear movement from limitations to cause and effect
- Use of long complex and compound sentences to convey complex thinking and information
- Critical use of contrast words
- Use of quotation marks
- Use of loaded words
- Use of imagery of light
- Use of metaphor
- Use of 'we' to connect writer and reader re the former's views
- Use of a variety of figurative devices (e.g., pun, metaphor) to make specific points
- Present a chronological outline of the development

2014

- Similes
- Personification
- Hyperbole
- Metaphor
- Visual imagery
- Contrast
- Repetition
- Understatement
- Narrative/descriptive prose
- Use of literary allusion
- Oxymoron / paradox

- Use of emotive words to create particular moods
- Direct repetition
- Use of a mixture of narration of events and reflection
- Short paragraphs
- Spatial sequencing of the narrative events to evoke various attitudes and emotions
- Locating of narrative reflection in a specific context
- Use of inductive / deductive ordering of events
- Use of I-narration to evoke pathos
- Narrative as anecdote

2015

- Provision of evidence to support the resurgence of local industry (the establishment of the Trinidad and Tobago Film Company; the introduction of an undergraduate degree in film at the University of The West Indies) to add to the credibility of the information presented.
- Contrast to highlight the resurgence of the local and regional film industry
- Chronological overview of films produced in the Caribbean from 1970 to present day which shows the developments in the industry.
- Examples of Hollywood blockbuster movies such as 'Jaws' and 'Star Wars' in an effort to substantiate the point that was being made.
- Examples and historical records of some films produced in the Caribbean since 1970 – to show the beginnings of the industry.
- Details of what led to the struggles in the industry – to show the decline in the industry. For example, "much of the region's top filmmaking talent struck out for greener pastures due north". "the surge in the popularity of television, with the attendant revolution in video production."
- Statements by an expert in the field – to substantiate the claim of resurgence in Caribbean cinema – for example, "How, with digital video and high-definition video, we're having a renaissance in filmmaking."
- Explanation of the cause of the resurgence – for example "One of the main reasons for this is purely practical: the technology has changed," "the advent of digital technology – vastly cheaper than film – has put movie cameras into the hands of more would-be filmmakers than before"
- Examples of Caribbean islands that were involved in this resurgence – to show that the resurgence was Caribbean wide, for example, "Trinidad and Jamaica"
- Italicized titles – to identify/classified films

- Short paragraphs – for ease of processing
- Jargon associated with film industry.
- Formal academic English with long sentences and complex syntax; academic vocabulary
- Dispassionate tone – to allow the reader to focus on the information and the story and to invest the text with seriousness or credibility
- Descriptive terms – to highlight the changes that took place in the film industry, for example, 'petered', 'ideological'
- Words and phrases that signal location in time- to capture the chronology of events, for example, 'was a time', 'now, however,' 'will one day'

46.   WORD SEARCH ACTIVITIES FOR ALL MODULES

MODULE ONE: GATHERING and PROCESSING INFORMATION

MODULE ONE:

GATHERING and PROCESSING INFORMATION

```
L R E T Y U I O P A T A D L A C I R O T S I H G H J D S S K
Y A I P A T A D Y R A D N O C E S R E D P O P U L A T I O N
F D N M N B V C E S R D F L H T N E M U R T S N I S E F F O
W E D G D R E S E A R T H I N T E R P R E T I V E S G O P I
T S U B U R E H O N G N G N D S L S V F E U G I V N J C T T
R C V B N A U J U H F I O T S V P L Y I G R G C K M R U E C
I R T R R M G E N U T I U E I E M E A N P E L E C V T S R E
N A S C D F G E H J K L P R D E A N D J T I K D Z E F G W L
I S H G R I P S T P E R T V E U S A L A K H G E Z R G R S L
D O O T A N N E J E K J B I W I V R R E N B E S U S B O G O
A D E R R H O E H R C H L E A P Q T A W L A D S J E C U I C
D A T E L I I D F S D H N W L Q S O B A B E L E I E X P R A
A E S T H E T I C U U F N S K L C U A S D R L Y E S J S T T
A Z X C V B A F E A M V N I A P U T Z X C V B N S D B E D A
H U C V B H V D S S H P O N Q O T E N E D B N M X I A Y E D
S D E R T Y R G H I Z X O C V U E A S D F G H J K L S K G H
C V B N M I E O Y V E I D F T Y E U I O L P R E F A C E E T
O S D F G H S J K E T L M N V B C S S A D R E X S D F E N T
M Z X C V B B N M A J G F E V I T A R R A N S P A C B Z E G
M U H B V F O M Z C L A S S I F I C A T I O N O C G H U R O
U S D X F E V I T A T N E M U G R A H U J K L S C F R E A E
N C X D R E N A S D F G F L K J G F T Y D S E I V C B N R V
I I S E A A G T Y H Y R F N Z X X S S D D A A T G A R B I I
C T B E G S I N N I N G E E N T E R N O N E S O V E F D S T
A S U R V E Y E E X P E R I M E N T S D E G Y R F G H R A C
T I O D N C T Y E N E M E Y A R D P R I M A R Y D A T A T E
I T C G D F G H J K K L N D E B N Y T C F P I L A S D G I L
O A S B C R Y B A B Y F T R A N S I T I O N W O R D S R O F
N T E R T V R E Y Y T I D I L A V D S F G A E B D R G F N E
S S E R I A N N O I T S E U Q I D S Y T I L I B A I L E R
```

AESTHETIC	INSTRUMENT	QUESTIONNAIRES
ANALYSIS	INTERPRETIVE	REFLECTIVE
ARGUMENTATIVE	INTERVIEWS	RELIABILITY
CLASSIFICATION	LANGUAGE TECHNIQUES	RESEARCH
DATA COLLECTION	NARRATIVE	SAMPLE
EFFERENT	OBSERVATION	SECONDARY DATA
EXPERIMENTS	ORGANIZATIONAL STRATEGIES	STATISTICS
EXPOSITORY	PERSUASIVE	SURVEY
FOCUS GROUPS	POPULATION	SYNTHESIS
GENERALIZATION	PREFACE	TRANSITION WORDS
HISTORICAL DATA	PRIMARY DATA	VALIDITY

MODULE TWO:

LANGUAGE and COMMUNITY

```
Q W E R T Y Y G O L O H P R O M M C O D E S W I T C H I N G
S G T Y U I O P C I M A N Y D E G X F S E E Y S Y N T A X U
D F G S T A N D A R D E N G L I S H E R D S B J I R D S H J
Z X C V B N M J K F R S X Z A D Y M B C V S A E E T R Y U O
S F G R H V X Z D I A L E C T K G P L K M V F R O Z E N E N
N H F S E D U T I T T A D F H O A F R O H A I R S T G R O O
S D A R T O R H U I L F F O R M A L I T Y D U R I N U G T I
E F B M A S L P T I V Z X S E Y T I N U M M O C R Y L P O T
N Y H U I L L E F N U E A S D F G B H D F O R A G E A E R P
V C O M M U N I C A T I V E B E H A V I O U R S E A T R U E
M E N P A S T E R O N C E I N T T S Y E D A B U H K O F G C
S D R G H F G H J K N G X E T A M I T N I N U A I O R P E R
V I T B R O T H E R V T C X Z A U C W Q U I T L E R Y I P E
U N R G A T N Y A T C H I Z X C T L A N O I T A R U T A M P
E T I I T L T O D R E T C N V B N L M K H J G F D S R E W T
L E N N H Y E S L I S E R T U D F R U I T L O O P S S E R H
A R I F B E U I F O G H J I L U Q W E S R Y T H Y O U I H G
T A D O P H Y H A S G C V I B E M H D B N M K Z L R E S T I
N C A R F H R S F C H Y T C E L O R C A J O D E W N S E T H
E T D M S K A D Z X C V B N N M H F D S T Y C D B S T L E L
M I A A Y F R T L A N G U A G E W C Y R E T A S F A I Y S A
U O N L H V T O U T A R T E F A C T S W V G U N B D O R D M
R N D T J P I I N F P L M N D F T C E L I S A B I W S A F R
T A T I O W B H H D U I E V I T A M R O F N I A S H R L T O
S L O M N E R P A R A L A N G U E I N A A C P O P U F U Y F
N A B E D S A D S E D F R T Y U E V I T A N I G A M I B Y T
I N A S F A S C I M E X O R P R B F A S D G H J L A S A U Y
L E X I C O N D G B J K L H C H R O N E M I C S G N D C I U
O N G N E F X T C V V N Y R E G I S T E R S A D S X C O K I
C I T S I R U E H A C X O N O N V E R B A L Z X C G P V L P
```

ACROLECT	FORMAL	VOCABULARY
ARBITRARY	FROZEN	LEXICON
ARTEFACTS	HEURISTIC	ATTITUDES
BASILECT	IMAGINATIVE	PERCEPTION
CASUAL	INFORMATIVE	LANGUAGE
CHRONEMICS	INSTRUMENTAL	MESOLECT
CODE SWITCHING	INTIMATE	NON VERBAL
COMMUNICATIVE	INTERACTIONAL	PROXEMICS
BEHAVIOURS	MATURATIONAL	REGISTER
CONSULTATIVE	PHONOLOGY	REGULATORY
CREOLE CONTINUUM	MORPHOLOGY	STANDARD
DIALECT	SYNTAX	VERBAL
DYNAMIC	SEMANTICS	VOCALICS

MODULE 3:

SPEAKING and WRITING

```
M N B G T E C H N O L O G Y E R T Y U I C H A N N E L O P G
G H O S T S T U N O I T A T E R P R E T N I D F G H J K O A
F E D I G I T A L D N T O B A G O Y S K O O B E C A F C V D
O N E D A Y A T A G T I M E D F G H J O I N I N G C L A S V
M E T G H O D L I O N O I T A Z I L A U T P E C N O C U R E
A X I N G O N A R E D R V I N G H O O D S T O R I E S E S R
U P E I P E P R M I N T S I N T E R N E T S N M C V F R S T
D A S D F M X U Z B M J L K S Y F R E D C K C A B D E E F I
I D G O A G H T H B I M V E R U G R E C E I V E R D S E R S
O X N C C Z F L B N A K L G F T A U Y J K I I O C L P H D E
V D I E I S T U S W T R Z E R O D L I D Y N A M O C A S K M
I F D D L D G C C E H V R E M O L D A R N S G J M B S J I E
S B O H I K U R L R E C X I D E S O U I J H D B P B Z B E N
U J C R T Y K E K T R D C J E K L E S A D E R I L C X D R T
A K N I A T J T J L S H V E D R U E T H O S S N E A E S F T
L L E Y T E P N H Y O G B F E H S C L W R T Y T M N R H H L
S G H U O A K I G U F G N V N O P O A D A E P R E R A V J L
E A P E R C E P T I O N O D S J T M S A H J O A N E C I P A
R D S R S J L S F O R N J S M G K P O S G H I P T T C C G N
U G E Y T X L D S P O W N A I M U L P H G N K E A E E S R O
T V Y G I A A N A I G E R D S E Y E O L U O T R R R N X V S
S M T M E C E G T D H G A A F D G M R K G I Y S Y F T L Z R
E H O P O M D A F G A R S A E I G E P D E R W O G E U E W E
G F P G P B M P D T A T D W G U H N T I E U G N A L A R A P
J A U S L R W O S A S Y F E Y M I T B N P A S A G F T O U R
L K I A O D Q N G C F U R H J K F A Z X A P O L B G I N I E
N M N F Y H I Y J V H I T D E A M R A D T R E T S E N E Y T
S E N D E R T T R B G L Y D S F T Y B S H E R W Q Y G F G N
S D E N E R W M L J J P H M O R T Y U I O M I S T Y I O N I
V C O M M U N I C A T I O N P R O C E S S M A S K I N G S E
```

ACCENTUATING	ENCODING	INTERPRETATION
ADVERTISEMENT	ETHOS	INTRAPERSONAL
APPEALS	FACEBOOK	LOGOS
AUDIOVISUALS	FACILITATORS	MEDIUM
BARRIERS	FEEDBACK	PARALANGUE
CAMPAIGN	GESTURES	PATHOS
CHANNEL	INFORMATION	PERCEPTION
COMMUNICATION	OVERLOAD	PROPOSAL
PROCESS	INSTAGRAM	RECEIVER
COMPLEMENTARY	INTERCULTURAL	SENDER
CONCEPTUALIZATION	INTERNET	TECHNOLOGY
DECODING	INTERPERSONAL	VISUAL AIDS
DIGITAL		

SECTION D
SAMPLE ESSAYS

47.   SAMPLE ESSAYS FROM STUDENTS FOR ALL MODULES

SAMPLE ESSAYS FOR MODULE 1

SECTION A
MODULE 1- GATHERING AND PROCESSING INFORMATION

With close referencing to the given passage, write an essay, in no more than 500 words, in which you

(i) *State the writer's main idea and dominant purpose*
(ii) *Discuss the information which includes THREE organizational strategies and THREE language techniques used by the writer to achieve this purpose*
(iii) *Evaluate the validity of the information presented*

Total 25 marks

Students' response

The writer's main point is that British citizens should be very concerned about the increase incursion on their privacy by the setting up of surveillance cameras. The writer's main purpose on the other hand is to create awareness or to convince the British public that they should be alarmed by the fact that there has been a marked increase in the number of cameras that the government has been setting throughout the country. To achieve this purpose the writer uses various strategies and language techniques, some of which are repetition, use of authorities, citing credible sources and giving statistical data.

A dramatic opening *'It's an alarming prospect...'* helps that writer to achieve his purpose of creating that sense of alarm over the high handed way that the British government operated when they increased the number of surveillance cameras that they are putting up in strategic areas. It also helps the readers to understand that if it can happen in England it can happen anywhere.

Additionally the writer repeated made allusion to the George Orwell's satirical novel titled *"1984"*. In this context the repetition of an allusion is an effectively powerful language technique in that it is not only done for emphasis of his point but it also points the readers in the direction of the fact that in the novel 1984 Orwell makes the point that the concept of privacy that persons so rigorously guard *"simply does not exist"* once people allow the government to *'watch'* them via their surveillance cameras.

The third language technique that the writer utilizes in this excerpt is that of emotive words such as *"obsession" "contagious", "ominous", "alarming"* and *"unnerving"*. Emotive words when used serve as an effective medium for transmitting the feelings that the writer intend to pass on to the readers. For example obsession evokes in the reader the sense of the extent to which the government is obsessively driven to *"watch"* and know all the doings of the citizenry.

The writer's careful selection of language techniques only serve to add to the achievement of his purpose in that the reading audience was bombarded by the constant sense of fear, unease and threat that the setting up of these surveillance cameras created.

Reference to credible sources of international news and newspapers such as the BBC as an organizational strategy add to the reliability and validity of the information in that it leaves them with little reason to doubt. These credible sources have lent their voice to express their concern and warning of what will happen if this growth in spy technology which the writer refers to as *"The Big Brother"* syndrome of watching the every move of the citizenry.

By the same token the writer also refers to document that was drawn up by respected academics in the persons of Dr David Murakami Wood and Dr Kristie Ball as an organizational strategy to help achieve the purpose. The effectiveness of this strategy is that the mere fact that these professionals have presented documentation that reinforces both the writer's main point and purpose is enough to add to credibility and reliability to the information presented.

As it were with the writer's choice of language techniques so it were with his choice of organizational strategies these added to the effective achievement of purpose by giving legitimacy to the fear that the information evoked.

SECTION A
MODULE 1- GATHERING AND PROCESSING INFORMATION

With close referencing to the given passage, write an essay, in no more than 500 words, in which you

(i) *State the writer's main idea and dominant purpose*
(ii) *Discuss the information which includes THREE organizational strategies and THREE language techniques used by the writer to achieve this purpose*
(iii) *Evaluate the validity of the information presented*

Total 25 marks

Students' response

The writer's main point is the University of the West Indies plans to open an online *"fourth campus"* to increase its accessibility to CARICOM students may have been cause by increasing competition and the need to produce *"work ready"* graduates. The writer's purpose is to justify to the reader why the University of the West Indies found it necessary to open a *'fourth campus'*. The writer achieves this purpose by using various organisational strategies, language techniques and appropriate tone.

Firstly the writer uses the organisational strategy of problem and solution, an example of this is seen in the second paragraph where the problem is presented *"Mona campus has limited housing on campus and has the disadvantage of being far removed from Jamaica's rural areas"* and the solution is presented in the third paragraph *"UWI is planning to open a fourth campus- the one sited in the most accessible of places, cyberspace"*. This strategy is effective because by showing the problem that many CARICOM students face even if it is in just one CARICOM territory. The writer achieves his purpose because the reader is able to understand why it was important for UWI to open an online campus to improve its accessibility.

Along the same lines, the writer also gave the opinion of a reliable source in the person of *"Professor E. Nigel Harris, Vice Chancellor of UWI, on Monday announced ..."* This is effective because readers tend to believe the opinions of professionals whom they deem reliable and so the fact that Professor Harris not only made the announcement but he justified the reasons as creating accessibility and work ready graduates.

Similarly, the use of examples of the competing institutions that UWI is up against is another organisational strategy used. For example "the *Northern Caribbean University has had close to a fresh start as it is no longer saddled… and the University of Technology"*. The use of this example shows the reader how the improvement in other regional institutions can take away potential students from UWI. Therefore the reader understands why it was important for UWI to improve its accessibility achieving the writer's purpose.

Additionally the writer uses the language technique of contrast in his quest to achieve his purpose. An example of this is seen in these words *'however"* and *"though"*. Its effectiveness is that contrast gives the readers the opportunity to see the issue from a different point of view thus helping the writer achieve his purpose of justification for a fourth campus.

Moreover the writer uses personal pronouns to include the audience as it encourages the reader to relate to what the writer is speaking about. This feeling of inclusion makes it easier for the writer to prove his point to the reader why it is important for UWI to open a fourth campus. The supporting example is *"We cannot help thinking though…"*

Repetition in many instances is used for emphasis and for memorization of the word competition was additionally used as a language technique. For example *"We cannot help but thinking, though that competition is on part a catalyst for this development"* and *"How this competition will affect the cost of education and attendant opportunities remains to be seen"*. This is effective because it makes the word competition memorable in the reader's mind which in turn makes it easier for the writer to prove that competition was the reason for UWI opening another campus.

As a result of specific words and phrases used by the writer the tone of this piece is varied and can thus be defined as complex. For example initially in the paragraphs one and two there's a neutral or dispassionate tone moving into one of rationalization in paragraphs three to five then ending with that of a hopeful tone of more improvement made by the University in the future.

In conclusion the writer uses many organisational strategies, language technique and a tone in this extract. All these were effective because they all aided in achieving the writer's purpose.

SECTION A
MODULE 1- GATHERING AND PROCESSING INFORMATION

With close referencing to the given passage, write an essay, in no more than 500 words, in which you

(i)   *State the writer's main idea and dominant purpose*
(ii) *Discuss the information which includes THREE organizational strategies and THREE language techniques used by the writer to achieve this purpose*
(iii) *Evaluate the validity of the information presented*

Total 25 marks

Students' response

The main idea is that there will be a sudden rise in the surveillance and spy technologies in the United Kingdom due to terrorist attacks.

The writer's main purpose is to educate the reader about the sudden drive towards surveillance and spy technologies in the UK, as a result of terrorist attacks, the citizens would be under constant watch.

In portraying his purpose the writer implemented several organizational strategies which would aid him in making his piece effective. One such strategy that was implemented was quoting from a reputable source. This was seen when the claim made by editors - Dr David Murakami Wood and Dr Kirstie Ball, Open University Lecturer in Organization Studies was mentioned. As a result of quoting from these reputable sources, this aids the writer in portraying his purpose, as it demonstrates that whatever the writer is saying is valid and is not opinionated but rather have been tested by people of authority, thus adding reliability, as this would make the piece more effective, as the writer is able to quote from reputable sources that would back up what he is saying, therefore making the reader more prone to believe what is being said, and thus achieving the purpose of educating the reader about the sudden need for surveillance technologies in the UK as a result of the terrorists attacks, which would result in the citizens being under constant watch.

Additionally the writer also utilized the strategy of using historical data. Which was seen when reference was made to a novel written in 1984, and the society that existed in the novel in 1949. This is a very effective strategy as it enabled the writer to add credibility to his piece in the aspect that, the reader is able to easily check back the records to see and verify whether what the writer is saying is true, thus adding reliability and indirectly achieving the purpose of educating the reader about the sudden drive towards surveillance and spy technologies in the UK, as a result of terrorists attacks.

Consequently, a strategy that was also utilized was the use of narration. In which the writer's piece was portrayed in a story like manner. This strategy is very effective as narration usually tend to entertain the reader, and actually capture the attention of the reader, thus making it very effective as the writer would be able to easily put forward his purpose of the sudden drive towards surveillance and spy technologies in the UK as the reader would be more prone to being attracted to reading the piece as it is capturing their attention.

However the writer did not only implement organizational strategies to aid him in portraying his purpose, but the use of language techniques was also put into effect. One such technique that was used was the use of Personification. This was seen when it was said 'Big Brother is watching you '. The state was being called Big Brother and was given the human quality of watching, what this does is furthermore emphasize how the citizens are going to be under constant watch due to the need for the sudden rise in surveillance technologies as a result of the terrorist attacks. This technique is very effective, as it re-enforces the idea of what surveillance technology is used for, and demonstrates further that the citizens would be under constant watch.

Subsequently the language technique of short paragraphing was also used. This technique is very effective as it is more easier to read, and doesn't make the reader feel as though they have to wade through boring text,but rather creates some sort of suspense and actually would get the reader to finish reading the piece, therefore making this technique very effective as by means of getting the reader to finish reading the piece,the writer would have been able to portray his purpose about the sudden drive towards surveillance and spy technologies in the UK, as a result of terrorist attacks, the citizens would be under constant watch.

Consequently, a technique that was implemented was the use of a serious tone. What this does is imparts upon the reader the level of importance of what is written, and it reveals the writer's attitude and tone. Thus making it very effective as it would allow the writer to bring across his purpose about the sudden drive towards surveillance and spy technologies in the UK, as a result of terrorist attacks, the citizens would be under constant watch. Therefore with the use of the serious tone, the reader is more likely to believe what is being said by the writer thus making this technique very effective.

In conclusion the writer used several organizational strategies and language techniques in portraying his purpose of the sudden drive towards surveillance and spy technologies in the UK, as a result of terrorist attacks, the citizens would be under constant watch. The strategies used were quoting from a reputable source, use of historical data and narration. Techniques used were personification, short paragraphing, and use of a serious tone.

SECTION A
MODULE 1- GATHERING AND PROCESSING INFORMATION

With close referencing to the given passage, write an essay, in no more than 500 words, in which you

    (i)   *State the writer's main idea and dominant purpose*

    (ii) *Discuss the information which includes THREE organizational strategies and THREE language techniques used by the writer to achieve this purpose*

    (iii) *Evaluate the validity of the information presented*

Total 25 marks

Students' response

The writer's main point is about George Washington, a founding father of the United States of America and also one of the greatest ever Americans, visit's to Barbados and the comparison made between United States of America and Barbados. His purpose is to inform the readers of George Washington, a founding father of the United States of America and also one of the greatest ever Americans, visits to Barbados and the comparison made between United States of America and Barbados.

Firstly, as an organizational strategy he implements examples and illustrations. "George Washington's monumental contribution to the American Revolution, the resultant Declaration of Independence, the establishment of the Bill of Rights, and his inauguration as the first President of the United States of America." This example shows examples of what George Washington achieved, justifying his greatness. In doing so, it aids the writer in achieving his purpose of informing the readers of George Washington, a founding father of the United States of America and also one of the greatest ever Americans, visit's to Barbados and the comparison made between United States of America and Barbados.

Additionally, compare and contrast as a next organizational strategy is used. "In these modern times when the United States of America is widely recognized as being the world's leading super-power and Barbados, by comparison, is considered something of a tiny speck on the surface of the globe, it is very challenging to conceive that 250 years ago this was not the case at all..." This example is effective in helping the writer achieve his purpose as it compares the size of the United States of America to that of Barbados.

Another organizational strategy used is historical data. "Nevertheless, it is a fact that when 19 year old George Washington came to Barbados in November 1761 from his home on the Potomac River in Virginia, he left behind a fledgling and relatively undeveloped colony and found himself in a new and exciting, more advanced world of innovative development and cultural sophistication." This helps in achieving the writer's purpose as it provides the reader with dates from the past which shows that the writer has done his research, allowing the readers to believe in his work.

Furthermore, the writer uses language techniques to achieve his purpose. One such language technique is tone. The tone seen in the extract can be described as an academic tone. The vocabulary used throughout the extract shows a high level of academic intelligence, for example, "Yet, whereas his heroic exploits and presidential tenure have been extensively chronicled and are therefore well known, it is not common knowledge that the one and only place that George Washington ever visited outside of America was here, the island of Barbados." This keeps the readers interested in his work due to the academic tone used, allowing his purpose of informing the readers of George Washington, a founding father of the United States of America and also one of the greatest ever Americans, visit's to Barbados and the comparison made between United States of America and Barbados, to be achieved.

Also, he implements personification as another language technique, "Combined with the British drive to encourage trade with and between its colonies," is an example of this. It compares the British to having a drive that encourages trade. By doing so, this comparison gives human-like qualities to Britain. This aids the writer in achieving his purpose.

Lastly, another language technique that is used is exaggeration. "He will always be remembered in the annals of history as one of the greatest ever Americans." The writer places emphasis on the greatness of George Washington and this achieves the writer's purpose.

This piece can be considered reliable since the writer uses facts and historical data based on events that have happened to bring out the achievements of George Washington.

SECTION A
MODULE 1- GATHERING AND PROCESSING INFORMATION

With close referencing to the given passage, write an essay, in no more than 500 words, in which you

(i) *State the writer's main idea and dominant purpose*
(ii) *Discuss the information which includes THREE organizational strategies and THREE language techniques used by the writer to achieve this purpose*
(iii) *Evaluate the validity of the information presented*

Total 25 marks

Students' response

The writer's main point is that there's a glaringly low level of content on news broadcasts which can be branded or classified as actually being news.

His main purpose is to illustrate what subjects are predominant in terms of the composition of the news broadcasts studied and at the same time drive home the point that a significant proportion of the news programme disseminated in fact steers clear from reporting news or is devoid of real news related content. In communicating the central idea of the excerpt and achieving his desired purpose, the writer employs certain strategies and language techniques aimed at improving the reader's response to the article and better capture the essence of it.

One such strategy is the use of statistical data. By referencing statistics pertaining to the composition of these newscasts such as only 41.3% of the programs contained news and commercials 30.4%, the writer solidifies and fortifies the credibility of the claims presented in the article and also lends of an air that the writer well versed in what he/she speaks of. Consequently, there's an inclination on the audience's part to take the claims of the reader with an elevated degree of seriousness and thus this peaks their intent to pay attention and show interest in the article. This obviously enables the transference of the writer's central message to the reader that real news content is significantly depleted. We further see a deeply lodged lamentation on the writer's part when he/she views as a positive thing, the fact that journalists and viewers see the need for change. The input of statistical data showcasing firsthand the reality lures the audience into grasping a greater appreciation of his/her prevailing sentiments and that there indeed exists a genuine basis for his/her frustration.

Another strategy implemented is the use of the cliché, 'If it bleeds, it leads' which effectively serves to capture and pique the audience's attention levels to particular points inserted in the article. Essentially, what the writer does through this cliché is to show the extent to which television stations will go to sensationalise even the newscast which should be serious in it content.

In addition, the use of the rhetorical question is evident in this article. Questions like 'What makes up the rest of the newscast?" and 'what stories make up actual news?', the writer in essence engages the reader's attention persuasively as well as his thought which is an instrument for instilling the writer's central idea in the mind of the reader. While the questions posed contain obvious, implied answers, it allows for the writer to shape and structure his points and information more effectively which is visually appealing to the reader and by providing the answers immediately after is a stimulant for swaying the reader to seeing things from the writer's perspective thus facilitating the achievement of his purpose.

The strategies and techniques employed in this article are all effective as they work together to highlight the main purpose that the dissemination of news related content on the studied news broadcast is surprisingly and that the real expected purpose of news themed programmes has eroded to an extent.

SAMPLE ESSAYS FOR MODULE 2

SECTION B
MODULE 2- LANGUAGE AND COMMUNITY

In an ESSAY of no more than 500 words, discuss the following:

a) *The differences in language in stanzas one and two*
b) *The attitudes to Standard English and Creole as revealed in the poem*
c) *How a televised reading of this poem could enhance it meaning*

Students' response

This essay attempts to discuss the differences in languages in the poem, the attitudes that persons may have and exhibit about languages such as Creole and Standard English and concludes with how a televised reading of the poem would enhance its meaning.

Generally, the type of language utilized by individuals is influenced by factors such as the context, the audience, the content or message and the registers created by it. In the case of *"A Tale of Two Tongues"* an interpersonal context exists between Ida and God and a formal register was created. In most situations, Standard English is used when addressing important individuals who should be spoken to with utmost respect. The first stanza is filled with religious imagery when Miss Ida was discussing the language that she used when speaking to God alone *"the language of holy things"*. She seemingly spoke only English to God as the content of her *prayers* was holy and she was addressing a *being* far *superior* to herself whom she says *"deserves a grammar of respectability"*. In the second stanza Miss Ida uses Creole as it is customarily used in informal contexts when the content of the conversation is not of a serious nature. Ida believed that Creole is appropriate for addressing *"fellow mortals"* and market vendors and for gossiping. The difference is glaringly obvious between the two languages that Miss Ida uses.

Attitudes to language are typically influenced by several factors such as social, historical, political and cultural factors. From the poem it is seen that Ida has a positive attitude towards English and she thinks of it with reverence as she refers to it as *"the language of holy things"*. This could be due to the fact that Standard English is often viewed as a superior language one befitting to communicate to the ultimate superior being called God. She also said that English had a *"grammar of respectability"* as if implying that Creole did not. Her attitude towards Creole was negative. She referred to it as *"the language of the labrish"* and *"the tongue of the markets and fields"*. Judging from these opinions it is clear that she thought Creole was far inferior to English. To her it was a lowly language used by common folk for less important matters. She also associated Creole with laughter and suffering and it was no problem for her to code switch to creoles when talking to regular people and back to English when worshipping God.

Additionally, a televised reading of this poem would greatly enhance the meaning as it would reveal activities such as the reader's hands and facial expression that indicate the formality and stiltedness of Standard English. The reader in the second stanza could do a mime of the emotions associated with the common things of life. A televised reading of this poem can reveal the writer's subtle suggestion of that Creole is a vibrant language and that Standard English is a conservative language of our colonial masters.

SECTION B
MODULE 2- LANGUAGE AND COMMUNITY

In an ESSAY of no more than 500 words, discuss the following:

a) *The differences in language in stanzas one and two*
b) *The attitudes to Standard English and Creole as revealed in the poem*
c) *How a televised reading of this poem could enhance it meaning*

Students' response

In this poem, one can clearly see that the writer employed both the Standard English in stanza one in its entirety as well as in stanza two. The glaring difference lies in the fact that stanza 2 is littered with specks of Jamaican Creole English. It can be deduced that he deliberately utilized Creole in stanza 2 to illustrate and emphasize that it was suitable mode of parlance granted the informal situation and setting which the poet painted of the markets and fields. Conversely, we immediately grasp the contrast as Stanza 1 is not flavoured with any sort of Creole, again possibly a purposeful ploy to demonstrate that matters of religion warranted the use of the more highly regarded Standard English.

It is well known that the Creole language is deemed a backward and broken down form of language mainly used for informal situations compared to its counterpart, Standard English which is held in high esteem and considered appropriate for formal settings. The poem, though revealing Ms Ida's beliefs could not capture this point more perfectly. Miss Ida firstly gives the perception that Standard English is a language associated with superiority and that it is the more respected, glorified form of language. This is symbolised through the statement 'the giver of commandments deserves a grammar of respectability.' However, it is not to say that her attitude promoted the suppression or stifling of Creole but rather that talking to God merited the use of the more polished, highly recognized Standard English because religion commands a profound level of formality.

In addition, her association of Creole to markets and fields shows her belief that this language is ideally suitable for more casual and informal settings and when it comes to the use of Creole that is how far the line stretches. On this end, she warmly embraces the language and doesn't view it with resentment or shame. On the contrary, her repugnance to use Creole with regard to religious matters can perhaps be labelled an adopted attitude influenced by the ingrained perception that the language is seen as inferior and not to mention inappropriate in the presence of God.

It is widely known a televised reading can enhance the meaning of the poem in that it allows for the audience to see the non verbal communications which took place, mainly the body language, gestures and facial expression of the central character, Miss Ida. For example, the viewing audience will notice an added air of vibrancy when Miss Ida uses Creole and in contrast the setting would be expectedly more serene in the presence of God. Essentially, it serves as a visual stimulus to the various settings in the poem: the market, the church and the way in which the characters presented themselves. Other aspects of non verbal communication, such as vocalic and elements of paralanguage such as tone, volume, pitch and rate, previously omitted, would be introduced and emphasized in the televised reading.

Indeed, it can be said that people's formulated attitudes to language fuel their motivation and choice of language. In this instance, Miss Ida's choice is motivated by the varying situations/settings which she confronts in her life and she adapts accordingly based on her systematic framework of beliefs. Making a language choice should be someone's prerogative but in many cases the choice comes about as a result of a negative perception against the language not chosen. Even though Miss Ida is open minded to using both forms of language, she is still guilty of this, for example, she perceives Creole to be a pronounced mark of disrespect to God.

SECTION B
MODULE 2- LANGUAGE AND COMMUNITY

In an ESSAY of no more than 500 words, discuss the use of language in the excerpt, focusing on the following:

(i)   *The varieties of language used by Harris and Five and what they reveal about each character*
(ii)   *What you notice in the relationship between Harris' verbal and non-verbal communication and his character.*

Students' response

Language plays an integral role in the communication process as it allows for effective communication to take place. In this excerpt, one can see that the writer employed both the mesolectal variety of Creole and the Standard English possibly a British variety. Through the writer's use of language, one can also see how people's perception of the use of language varies. In understanding the role of language, further analysis into the varieties of language used by both Harris and Five as well as Harris' verbal and non-verbal communication is necessary to reveal certain aspects about the characters.

Initially, the writer introduces Harris as a man who likes English customs. He describes various activities that Harris mimics in an attempt to seem more like an Englishman. As such, Harris uses British Standard English to add to his appearance as an Englishman. His speech contains the presence of auxiliary in present continuous tense, for example, *'I'm going.'* The use of this language is quite appropriate given the length of time spent in Britain.

However, Harris is from the Caribbean and at no point in time does he use the Creole language. This indicates that Harris is ashamed of his Caribbean identity. It is also indicative of his belief that using Standard British English will help him to progress in his everyday life whereas using the Creole language would only hinder his self-development.

Additionally, Harris' use of Standard English stems from his association with the "bigshots" in his effort to be like them. It shows his belief that Standard English is superior to the Creole language and hence his use of Standard English allows him to work with "bigshots". Five thinks Harris' behaviour is false, opportunistic, and snobbish.

Contrastingly, Five uses Trinidadian mesolectal Creole throughout the extract as seen in the absence of auxiliary in, *'you looking'; 'things going'*. This reveals that he is from Trinidad and that he is proud of his Caribbean identity. Unlike Harris, Five uses the Creole language in the presence of Harris' *"distinguished"* guests at the fete. This shows that whilst he is unashamed of his heritage and does not believe that Standard English is superior to Creole he is also pointedly speaking in Creole to aggravate Harris. Five therefore does not have the same attitude to language as Harris.

Similarly Harris' choice of language, his verbal and non-verbal communications are also indicative of his perceptions and beliefs. As Harris walks upright with a bowler, umbrella and a briefcase it shows that he exudes pride in his likeness to an Englishman. In trying to seem more like an Englishman, Harris shows extreme politeness by *buying flowers for the Lord's daughter* and *giving up his seat* to allow women to sit on the bus. All of these actions of politeness and his mimicking of the behaviour of Englishmen illustrate his belief that being English is superior.

Harris is wary of Five and this is seen by him *keeping an eye out* for him. He believes that Five carries about himself in an improper way and tries to correct him by telling him *"comport yourself properly"*. Harris' actions of warning Five and *looking around desperately* affirms his character's position of abject discomfort whenever Five is around him. This illustrates that he is ashamed and at times even disgusted with his Caribbean background.

In conclusion, this excerpt illustrates that the varieties of language as well as verbal and non-verbal communication are common denominators in highlighting the attitudes and perceptions that characters possess towards language.

In an ESSAY of no more than 500 words, discuss the use of language in the excerpt, focusing on the following:

(i) *The relationship between the writer's use of language and the context of the narrative*
(ii) *The appropriateness of the narrator's language*
(iii) *Whether Pinkie's language was motivated by linguistic and/or non linguistic factors*
(iv) *Ways in which a video presentation of this interaction would help to highlight the fact that these are Caribbean speakers communicating in a Caribbean setting.*

Total 25 marks

Students' response

Language is an integral component, always present in the way human beings communicate. In properly understanding language and its multiple uses, it is important to first take into consideration, relationships of persons and the context of communication, dialectal variations and their appropriateness, linguistic and non-linguistic factors, and ways in which to enhance delivery and understanding through use of a video presentation.

Primarily, it can be noted that context of communication can influence greatly the register that is created while communicating and as a result, the type of language used. Hence, in this context, set in a beauty parlour on an island, indicating an interpersonal context, it is safe to note that the register created in this instance was a casual one and thus, Creole was used instead of Standard English. This was due to the fact that the setting was such that individuals who are familiar with one another, for instance Miss Daisy and Pinkie meet and interact in this environment. It serves as an arena for communication and *"gossip"* for those of the area. Therefore, it is understood that one would use their own casual and native language, Creole, when expressing themselves in such a comfortable context.

Furthermore, many factors such as background or origin and social status influence the type of language one uses. Thus, the writer's use of Creole was soundly justified. Being a native of a small developing island, the writer would have grown up speaking Creole and would have been habitually exposed to Creole and its use. It will therefore seem natural and comfortable to the writer to use the language she knows well in order to properly express herself. Additionally, it can be seen from the extract that the writer does not have a high level of social status as indicated by her statement *"is the only place we have for we-selves"* in lines 11-12. She does not have much exposure, if any at all, to regions outside the sanctity of her little island, therefore, it would seem odd to her to speak a language that is not native of her island.

On a separate note, it can be noted that various linguistic factors such as grammar, phonology and vocabulary as well as non-linguistic factors for example, shows of emotion and exposure to more-developed nations greatly influence one's use of language. Pinkie uses Standard English most times when speaking in the extract but code-switched two Creole twice in the extract. In sudden shows of emotion such as in line 1 *"That's why this country will nevah get ahead, nevah get ahead"* and in line 17 *'Guess wha', Miss Daisy, 'Guess wha'?'* In line 1, the emotions expressed are of anger and frustration with the state of affairs in the island and in line 17, she expresses excitement about something she has been waiting for and received. When expressing oneself, one tends to use a language most familiar to them and one that can ensure proper expression of their emotions.

Additionally, Pinkie's use of Standard English was demonstrated by her use of grammar rules, subject –verb agreement, in line 5 *"there wasn't one power cut"* as well as the phonology present in her speech in line 15 *"To tell you the truth"*, she pronounces her *"th"* sounds as one would in Standard English rather than simply using *"d"* or *"t"* as in Creole. Her use of Standard English was also motivated by the fact that she visited America where the first language is Standard English. She thus saw this language as the superior one and dismissed the use of Creole. The difference in her language before and after visiting America can be seen in the extract by her use of Creole in lines 20-24 before going to England and in lines 4-7 where she complains about the island, comparing it to England during her stay there in Standard English. Though Pinkie tries to speak in Standard English only after returning from England, her use of vocabulary reveals a sense of Creole originally present in her speech, where in line 5 where Pinkie uses *"whole"* to mean *"entire"*.

In conclusion, video presentations allow the audience to experience many aspects of this communication process which they would have otherwise missed completely or partially. For instance, the casual register created in this scene would be effectively highlighted by re-creating the scene by use of props in the video, depicting to the audience clearly proxemics which would indicate a familiar relationship between the two speakers, the dress of the characters as well as facial expressions of Miss Daisy and Pinkie to convey to the audience the emotions of the characters, emotions of excitement, frustration, and annoyance on the part of Miss Daisy. Furthermore, the audience will be able to hear the difference in Pinkie's speech, that is, when she code switched from Creole to Standard English and vice verse, to effectively understand the difference of the two languages. Thus, the audience gains a deeper understanding of the language that originates from the Caribbean, Creole.

SECTION B
MODULE 2- LANGUAGE AND COMMUNITY

In an ESSAY of no more than 500 words, discuss the use of language in the excerpt, focusing on the following:

(i) *The relationship between the writer's use of language and the context of the narrative*
(ii) *The appropriateness of the narrator's language*
(iii) *Whether Pinkie's language was motivated by linguistic and/or non linguistic factors*
(iv) *Ways in which a video presentation of this interaction would help to highlight the fact that these are Caribbean speakers communicating in a Caribbean* setting.

Total 25 marks

Students' response

In this essay, I will be looking at the relation between the writer's use of language and the context, the appropriateness of the language, whether the choice of language is motivated by linguistic or non-linguistic reasons, and finally how a video presentation can enhance the interaction between the two characters.

A writer's language choice is usually influenced by numerous factors including the audience, content, perception of the language and the context. The context or situation is a very important factor when choosing a language. In Alecia McKenzie's story, *"Pinkie"*, the context of the narrative is a casual setting in a beauty parlour where two friends are having a conversation. Since the context is a casual one and the characters are familiar with each other, the writer uses Creole, which is the characters' native language, within an informal register.

Generally, when evaluating the appropriateness of the choice of language, factors such as the context, audience and content must be considered. In this case, the narrator's language choice, which was Creole, was indeed appropriate. As stated previously, because the context is a beauty parlour and a casual conversation between friends, Creole is appropriate as the situation is a casual one and both characters appear to be familiar with one another. Furthermore, because her audience, Pinkie, is her friend and they are both West Indian, it is appropriate to use Creole as they both understand the language and they have a friendly relationship. In addition, since the content is not serious and is a casual conversation, Creole is appropriately used. Also, some of the content is complaining therefore Creole is appropriate since West Indian people often use Creole to express their emotions when they are distressed.

An individual's choice of language is usually motivated by either linguistic or non-linguistic reasons. Many times in the Caribbean, people's choice of language especially that of a foreign language are due to non-linguistic reasons. In this instance, Pinkie chooses to speak British Standard English *"nevah"* for non-linguistic reasons such as having spent some time in England for a period of time and also just because she is frustrated and angry that her birth country *"would nevah get ahead"*, and *"can't hold its head above water"* These reasons are non-linguistic and does not give Pinkie the linguistic ability to speak British Standard English. Pinkie chooses to speak Standard English when she speaks about visiting England since she perceives them as being a better and more advanced country, and she probably wants to speak like an *"Englishman"*.

In general, the use of video presentations can highlight and enhance the interactions of characters as it allows the audience to see the setting the characters are in, and the communicative behaviours displayed. In this situation a video presentation can allow the audience to see communicative behaviours displayed, for example artefacts around the beauty parlour that can highlight that they are Caribbean women in a Caribbean setting. Also during the scene where Pinkie is pacing up and down, a video presentation can allow us to clearly see her agitation and frustration. Not to mention we will be able to hear the disgust and scorn when Pinkie speaks about the sun being too hot in the Caribbean. Moreover, a video presentation of the scene where Pinkie tells Miss Daisy she is going to America would be beneficial as it her communicative behaviours such as her vocalics and proxemics can be shown, which enhances the piece.

SECTION B
MODULE 2- LANGUAGE AND COMMUNITY

In an ESSAY of no more than 500 words, discuss the use of language in the excerpt, focusing on the following:

(i) *The THREE factors which may have influenced the writer's choice of language*

(ii) *How the language of the dialogue reveals the nature of the relationship between Brackley and Teena*

(iii) *How would a directed film version of this dialogue highlight the emotions and attitudes displayed*

Total 25 marks

Students' response

In this essay we will be looking at the factors which may have influenced the writer's choice of language, how the language of the dialogue reveals the nature of the relationship between Brackley and Teena and finally, how filming of this episode will highlight the emotions and attitudes displayed.

A writer's choices of language are determined by different factors such as audience, content, context or to establish his identity. In Samuel Selvon's story *"Ways of Sunlight"* the chosen language of the narrative is Creole; the writer may have chosen this based on his intended audience which may have been Caribbean residents. Similarly, the writer may have also written in Creole to establish his identity as that of a Caribbean national.

The language of the dialogue reveals the nature of Brackley and Teena's relationship. Language has various functions such as expressing oneself, directing or informing. Language can be used to express one's feelings, ideas or attitudes without necessarily taking a reader into consideration. In this story Brackley and Teena's relationship is revealed through their dialogue in the story. Brackley's annoyance at Teena is expressed when he says *"What you doing in London?"*, *"What you come here for, eh?"* here his annoyance at Teena's arrival is clearly seen. However his concern for her is also expressed when he says *"What you think the Colonial Office is, eh? You think they will do anything for you?"* Similarly, Teena's reaction at Brackley's response to her arrival is also expressed: *"What happen, you buy the country already? You ruling England now? The queen's abdicate?"* Here it is seen that she is almost mocking Brackley for being annoyed at her. She shows him that she is not afraid of him and is standing up for her decision of following him to London. The language of the dialogue reveals that Brackley is annoyed at Teena's appearance in London and Teena's willingness to follow Brackley to London.

In conclusion, filming this episode can highlight various emotions and attitudes portrayed by the characters in the story. For instance, when Brackley *"hold his head and bawl"* the frustration and pain would be plainly seen on his face and expressed in his voice for the audience to witness. The body language and proxemics of Brackley and Teen while they were arguing should reveal their annoyance at each other, both of them should stand a little way off from each other, enough distance to highlight their frustration. Also, in the end when *"Brackley find himself holding onto Teena suitcase"* their proxemics should reveal that they made up in the end.

SECTION B
MODULE 2- LANGUAGE AND COMMUNITY

In an ESSAY of no more than 500 words, discuss the following:

(i)   *The dialectal variation used in the passage*

(ii) *The effect that B. Wordsworth has on: (i) the boy (ii) his mother*

(iii) *How film would effectively capture the communicative behaviours in this excerpt.*

Total 25 marks

Students' response

A speaker's choice of dialectal variation is influenced by various factors such as setting, audience, relationship with the other person just to name a few. In this excerpt from V.S Niapaul's Miguel Street we see the two dialectal variations of Standard English and Creole being utilised.

In this excerpt adapted from Naipaul's Miguel Street, one can see the usage of Trinidad Standard English as well as Creole were the predominantly employed forms of language by the protagonists presented. As far as the way the man spoke, he used the highly regarded Standard English throughout the excerpt. This is evidence that he is a more than respectably educated individual and the manner in which he is presented with regard to him being tastefully and tidily dressed is intended to give that impression as well.

On the other hand, Sonny and his mother's use of Creole mostly reflect the mesolect end of the continuum. However, Sonny can't be classified as completely uneducated as is evidenced in the opening line of the excerpt, perhaps he felt a greater sense of comfort using it in the casual setting of his home to his mother and Mr. Wordsworth. There is indeed a greater likelihood that Sonny's mother was deprived of an education, however, it can be said that her influence for using Creole not only stems from her lack of an educational background but cultural, geographic and the class of society she comes from as well which is the lower socio class. Both Sonny and his mother's language complied with typical Creole features, the most marked feature being the verbs not accommodating the English subject verb agreement rule. Examples include 'He say he want to watch' and 'he watch the bees'.

It can be seen from the beginning the man's presence evokes sentiments of bemusement, superstition and perhaps some fear which is indicated by his remark 'What you want?' Mr. Wordsworth's response only served to elevate these sentiments and quite expectedly and she is equally suspicious and uneasy about his presence thus provoking aggravation, aggression and hostility in how she responds to Mr. Wordsworth. She is generally disrespectful, holding no regard for Mr. Wordsworth, however her son shows some form of respect by refusing to tell him what his mother said, 'Tell that blasted man to haul his tail', perhaps because he was an adult figure.

We also note the lasting effect Wordsworth's use of language has on both individuals. He points out his mother's sense of worry and preoccupation with Wordsworth's use of Standard English highlighting the internal struggle to accept things which are alien or foreign to us. Sonny's description of Wordsworth's language as 'so good' illustrates a popular conception which associates Standard English with superiority, prestige and he is obviously mesmerized by this. A cloud of inferiority takes over both as Creole itself has its attached stigmas of being improper, inferior and sub standard.

It is widely known that film would greatly enhance the audience's ability to see the communicative behaviours as it acts as a visual stimulus to how the characters portrayed themselves in this regard. It allows for the audience to see non verbal elements such as facial expression, body language and gestures. For example, the viewing audience can see the mother's aggression levelled at Mr. Wordsworth and the accompanying facial expression because of the man's presence. Paralanguage such as volume, pitch, tone of the characters' input would be also emphasized and lastly their use of proxemics and space offer us through film another means to interpret and analyse their behaviours.

Essentially, film, in general, has the added visual dimension, which can reinforce the attitudes, behaviours of the characters in a more meaningful, effective manner and in a way which printed matter cannot. Visual material can therefore greatly improve a reader's understanding and appreciation of the excerpt.

SECTION B
MODULE 2- LANGUAGE AND COMMUNITY

In an ESSAY of no more than 500 words, discuss the following:

a) *The different ways in which the clerk and Tantie use language in the excerpt*
b) *The various social factors responsible for the noticeable tension between the clerk and Tantie*
c) *How a video presentation would highlight this tension*

Total 25 marks

Students' response

In the extract from Monica Skeet's story *"The Road"* the use of Creole and Standard English will be analysed according to the context it is used in, the social factors responsible for the tension in the interaction of the characters and lastly, the ways in which a video presentation will highlight that tension.

Language serves differing functions such as to express oneself, to persuade, to refuse and to inform. The two languages used in the extract are Standard English and Creole. Tantie speaks Creole and the chief clerk uses Standard English. They both utilize language differently in the situation. Tantie uses language to refuse and disapprove of the clerk's offer *"Me old home good enough..."* On the other hand the clerk uses language to persuade *"we'll fix you up nice and snug"* and to inform/warn *"you won't be able to stay there..."*

In general, the socially dominant group in society ensures that its dialect is the one that assumes the place of importance in society and is considered to be the standard language of that society; usually this language is Standard English. In this extract there are social factors present responsible for tension in the interaction between Tantie and the chief clerk. Additionally, in this excerpt there is interaction between people of significantly differing socio-economic statuses, the chief clerk of the office and Tantie who he remembers *"buying three oranges for a penny from Tantie's tray in the market"*, one reason for the tension may be that the chief clerk perceives himself as better than Tantie or of a higher social status than her and thus expects her to listen to him without putting up much of a fuss. Another factor may be that because of their use of differing languages, the clerk being a public servant is accustomed to speaking to clients in Standard English as seen in his interaction in the extract, and Tantie speaks to him in Creole, she may think that he is belittling her.

In conclusion, the use of video presentations can highlight and enhance the interactions of the characters, as it allows the audience to see the setting they are in; for example, in this extract objects around the office can highlight the social status difference between Tantie and the clerk. Also, during the scene where Tantie is walking up the steps of the Housing Office 'with great dignity' a video presentation will allow the audience to clearly see her body language such as the positioning of her head that allows for it to be described as *'with dignity'*. Also, the different tones of voice used by the clerk can be heard by the audience i.e. when he is speaking to his assistant and when he speaks to Tantie.

SECTION B
MODULE 2- LANGUAGE AND COMMUNITY

With close referencing to the passage, in an ESSAY of no more than 500 words, discuss the following:

(i) *Possible reasons for the writer's language choices used in the narrative*

(ii) *Difficulties that non-West Indians may experience in understanding the passage*

(iii) *How a video presentation could enhance the comedic effect of the extract.*

Total 25 marks

Student's response

This Olive Senior's extract titled, *"Do Angels wear Brassieres,"* that appeared in the 1977 Oxford Caribbean Short Stories describes the conversation between an Archdeacon and a young girl, Beccka who is preparing for her Confirmation, as well as the series of unfortunate but comical chain of events that followed once Beccka as what can only be considered as an 'eye popping, jaw dropping' question. This essay will discuss the reasons for the writer's language choices, the difficulties that non-West Indians may encounter in understanding the passage and will conclude with an analysis of how a video presentation will enhance the comedic effect of the passage.

When choosing languages in a specific situation, writers take into consideration various factors. In this case Olive Senior may have considered the Archdeacon's status in the community when she gave him Standard English as his language. This was a great choice as people generally expect a person in the Archdeacon's position to speak Standard English almost all the time rather than Creole, as seen in this example, '*Surely you must have some questions about doctrine, hm, religion, that puzzle you*'. In the same vein the Archdeacon must have attained tertiary level education thus again making the choice of Standard English a correct one, as it is the norm for the higher the level education of a person's education the high the possibility of that person speaking the Standard English.

People may expect Creole to be the language choice of young Beccka especially as in this case the narrator's voice when describing the other members of the household was definitely Creole. Unexpectedly though Beccka matched the Archdeacon with Standard English as seen in this example, "Sir, what I want to know is this for I can't find it in the Bible. Please sir, do angels wear brassieres?' As a child in conversation with an older person it is customary that she would show her respect for not only age but also in recognition of the office and position that the Archdeacon holds in the Christian community as emphasised when she addressed him as 'Sir'.

Short of sounding cliché, many persons still hold the belief that Creole is the language of comedy and the fact that there was the noticeable switched from Standard English to Creole when narrator related the events that followed when Beccka asked this adult and 'man of the cloth' a rather personal and embarrassing question, ...do angels wear brassieres?'. Undoubtedly Creole is the more effective of the two especially as the ensuing chain of events were really comical to the readers who could understand. Standard English could not have put life and comic relief to these events, *"Auntie Mary stopbraps in the doorway with fright when she hear Beccka's question. She stop so sudden that Cherry bounce into her and spill a whole pitcher of cold drink all down Auntie Mary back. As the coldness hit her Auntie Mary jump and half her tray throwaway on the floor. Milk and sugar and sandwiches a rain down on Archdeacon."*

Whilst as expected West Indians will have no problem understanding the nuances in this piece which will all be lost to a non- West Indian speaker. To the West Indian the word 'braps' describes the suddenness of at which Auntie Mary stopped upon hearing Beccka's question to the Archdeacon., on the other hand a non – West Indian will be totally clueless as this in not a word that they use or can look up in a regular dictionary. The lack of pluralisation of words is a common feature in a Creole speaker's speech and so they will understand the narrator when he says, 'Archdeacon <u>jump</u> up with his handkerchief and <u>start</u> <u>mop</u> himself...' or '... food and drink for ten <u>Archdeacon</u>,'. Finally, because a West Indian speaker can understand tenseless words does not mean that it's the same with a non-West Indian speaker. The latter may experience difficulties in understanding because there is no indication of when the event took place as seen in these examples, *'Auntie Mary jump...'* and *'...when she hear Beccka's question'*

Technology such as a video will indeed enhance the comedic effect of the extract. For example many features of the characters' body language can be observed thus enhancing the communication taking place, the Archdeacon can be seen eagerly sittin up and leaning forward awaiting Beccka's 'serious' question but once she utters it the camera can show the shock (jaws drops, eyes pop) on his face and the deflation in his posture. On Beccka the camera will zoom in on her face that is *'screwed up'* in supposed concentration but once she asks the question this look can be changed to supposedly innocent 'mischief'. Another comical situation that can be highlighted in the video presentation is the hilariously narrated scene, *...she stop braps'*, 'the cold pitcher that Cherry was carrying fell of Auntie Mary's back (she must have screamed and squirmed with the double shock) the food and drink for the Archdeacon ended up not in his stomach but on him and whilst this in any situation should not have caused relief it did in this case creating comedy. As the Archdeacon instead of being upset for the mess on his clothes he welcomed the confusion and may have seen it as 'God sent' as the look of ultimate was on his face. Finally, the comic relief can be seen when both Auntie Mary and the Archdeacon who ordinarily would never touch each other but in this case were busy trying to mop each other up and comically must have been touching in places that may seem inappropriate.

Conclusively, language choices used in the narrative were done so for several reasons known to the writer but because audiences vary there is the possibility that understanding and enjoying the piece may be difficult for the non West Indian section of the audience. In cases like this though a video presentation can in some way enhance the comedic effect.

SAMPLE ESSAYS FOR MODULE 3

SECTION C
MODULE 3- SPEAKING AND WRITING

Read the scenario below and answer the questions that follow.

There have been several deaths from some rare water borne disease in your village and the Ministry / Department of Health has embarked on a nationwide programme to advise the public of this disease and to recommend precautions which should be taken. The Ministry has sent you on this health campaign to a village which is cut off from the larger community and where most of the villagers have only basic skills in English.

 a. *Indicate an appropriate medium/channel that you would use to inform the villagers of this deadly threat.*
 b. *Compose your presentation.*
 c. *Write a paragraph explaining the appropriateness of your composition.*

Student's response

For this presentation I have decided to use a community meeting (to be held in the common space of the community centre) as the medium through which I will inform the villagers of the deadly water borne disease that has been plaguing their village. I think this medium is most effective as small villages tend to be tight knit communities and as such meetings are usually well attended.

Good afternoon residents of Ocoro village, I am Kathi Ann Williams and I am here on behalf of the Ministry of Health to share with you important information about the Crichlow virus that is now prevalent in this village.

The Crichlow virus is caused by tiny organisms that are currently living in the Tarouba River; these organisms cause deadly reactions once inside of the human body. The most common of these symptoms are high fever, vomiting and lack of appetite. If anyone of you experiences any of these symptoms you are advised to do two things; first you report it to the nearest health office and then you seek medical attention as quickly as possible.

In order to prevent the spread of this disease you are asked to not use water directly from any water sources for drinking, bathing or performing any household chores but rather either boil the water, treat it with household bleach or if you are able to purchase bottled water. It is extremely important that all villagers understand that the water sources would be treated for the next thirty days and that during that duration they should desist for using the water.

Conclusively, I believe this composition is appropriate because of the fact that it seeks to create much needed awareness of the severity of the situation that the villagers face. The use of a village meeting held at the community centre is a great idea as the campaign manager would be able to reach as many if not all the villagers at the same time and also as meetings go the structure would allow for both consultative and casual registers and also a mixture of Creole and basic Standard English. The use of Creole and basic Standard English is being sensitive to the fact that most of the villagers have only the basic skills. The consultative register would also facilitate the many questions that the villagers may be seeking answers for. Giving information like the symptoms and the precautions were appropriate because that was the main objectives of the campaign.

SECTION C
MODULE 3- SPEAKING AND WRITING

Read the scenario below and answer the questions that follow.

*There have been several deaths from some rare water borne disease in your village and the Ministry /
Department of Health has embarked on a nationwide programme to advise the public of this disease and
to recommend precautions which should be taken. The Ministry has sent you on this health campaign
to a village which is cut off from the larger community and where most of the villagers have only basic
skills in English.*

(a) *Indicate an appropriate medium/channel that you would use to inform the villagers of this
deadly threat.*

(b) *Compose your presentation.*

(c) *Write a paragraph explaining the appropriateness of your composition.*

Student's response

(a) An appropriate channel and medium that would be used to inform the villagers of this
deadly threat would be a face to face meeting, such as a community meeting. This is appropriate
because the language used would be understandable by most persons, even those with just basic
skills in English.

Good day ladies and gentlemen of Couva. My name is Rebecca Black and the Ministry of
Health has sent me on a health campaign. My purpose today is to advise you of a rare water-borne
disease in your territory and to recommend precautions which should be taken. As you may have
observed, your village has been cut off from the larger community. This was done to contain and
minimize the spread of the disease to other villages.

What are water-borne diseases? Water-borne diseases are caused by pathogenic
microorganisms that are transmitted in contaminated fresh water. They are extremely harmful
and lead to severe illness and may even be fatal. They work by lowering the body's resistance and
intake of nourishment, resulting in further infections and diseases. It is advisable that you do not
use the water in your taps, in nearby rivers, streams etc. since you can be infected while using the
water for your daily activities such as bathing, washing and in the preparation and consumption
of food.

I recommend that you follow these precautions to minimize your chances of contacting the
disease. You should only drink bottled or filtered water since other water sources are at high risk

of being contaminated, wash your containers daily, wash food properly before cooking and cook food at high temperature so as to kill harmful bacteria, avoid flies by disposing wastes properly, always keep foods and beverages covered, avoid swimming in rivers, lakes etc. The most important method of prevention is to wash your hands often, especially before preparing food and before eating.

If you notice that you may have been infected, please refrain from going to work, school etc. until the symptoms subside, thereby limiting the spread of the disease. Symptoms include watery-diarrhoea, flu-like symptoms, loss of appetite, cramps and nausea.

(b) The presentation is appropriate as it allows the villagers to have face to face interaction with the speaker and therefore allows immediate feedback. Therefore, if villagers have any questions and concerns, they can bring it to the speaker's attention.

SECTION C
MODULE 3- SPEAKING AND WRITING

Read the scenario below and answer the questions that follow.

Your Students' Council is on a drive to promote Peace and Love in Schools (PALS). As the President of the Council, you have been asked to address students who have just entered the first form of secondary school, on methods students can employ to demonstrate Peace and Love.

(a) *State the medium/channel you will use to present your message to these students.*
(b) *Compose your message.*
(c) *Write a paragraph explaining/justifying the appropriateness of your presentation.*

Students' response

As the President of the St Andrews High School Students' Council I have been asked by the administration to address my fellow form one students on methods that they can employ to promote Peace and Love in Schools (PALS).

Choosing the most effective medium is important in ensuring that this message reaches the audience of the form ones and as a result I chose to have direct contact via a morning assembly during the first week of school. This medium of the assembly would allow for me to utilize many options such as effective language, create casual and consultative registers and also use visual aids. The meeting will also afford me the opportunity for feedback and a chance to clarify any misconception that the students may have.

Good Morning, Madam Principal and Vice principal and students of St Andrews High especially the first formers, my name is Katherine Moll and I am the President of the Student Council here at this school. The Principal Mrs Chance has asked me to address you on the topic of Peace and Love in school and some of the various ways you the first formers can show peace and love to each other and by extension to all.

I am sure that every one of you love your parents or some member of your family, do you? So what would you say is love? For most people, love is kindness, compassion, and forgiveness for another person. An example of love is seen when your friend is struggling with a problem and tells you in secret, you as a friend will never tell anyone else. That is love! Love, is knowing that you will be a friend to someone in the class room when all others will not! Love is not gossiping about a classmate when others are doing so.

Love and peace are closely related. Peace is to avoid arguing and fighting. So how can you show peace and love to your schoolmates? Well you can begin by sharing, for example if someone forgets her lunch at home it would be selfish not to share with that person, wouldn't it? You are a peaceful person when you say kind words about each other. It's when you avoid calling people names despite how angry you may get because name calling can be hurtful and this neither display love nor peace. Gossiping is another act that you should desist from doing as it can destroy friendship and create very negative emotions which is not what PALS is all about. If you have to spread news please try spreading good news about your classmates and school mates!

There have been so many instances of school violence in our country in recent times and this of course is not encouraged in Peace and Love schools. If you ever see students fighting you should get the teacher or dean immediately. Please do not under any circumstances try to '*jump in*' to stop a fight! School violence is absolutely unacceptable and you will be suspended. If someone is taunting you the best thing to do is to ignore that person and if they persist then it's bullying and that is something that you should tell any teacher or even your parents about. In this school we want to practice peace and love and it begins with each one of you. It is your responsibility to be loving and peaceful and if you make a continuous effort then this school is going to be a PAL school.

In conclusion, my presentation is appropriate since I used simple language, gave many examples of how the first formers can practice peace and love in school. The vocabulary was simple so that they were able to understand. The channel chosen was ideal since an assembly allowed for face to face interaction and students would have been able to assess my enthusiasm and sincerity. Immediate feedback was aloes facilitated during assembly.

SECTION C
MODULE 3- SPEAKING AND WRITING

Read the scenario below and answer the questions that follow.

Your Students' Council is on a drive to promote Peace and Love in Schools (PALS). As the President of the Council, you have been asked to address students who have just entered the first form of secondary school, on methods students can employ to demonstrate Peace and Love.

(a) *State the medium/channel you will use to present your message to these students.*
(b) *Compose your message.*
(c) *Write a paragraph explaining/justifying the appropriateness of your presentation.*

Students' response

The medium that would be used is a morning assembly with all the first formers. In this assembly I will also have use of a PowerPoint as a visual aid containing pictures to support the examples of methods that demonstrate peace and love in school.

Good morning everyone, my name is Anisha Babwah it's an honour to be back at my alma mater to address the students of Form 1. I am here to promote PALS, the acronym for Peace and Love in Schools. During my 15 minute presentation I will give you information about some of the methods that you the first form students can use to promote and practice peace and love not only in the school but also outside as well.

First, I will begin by defining and giving examples of the terms Peace and Love. What is Peace? How do we recognize a peaceful person and situation? Well for many of us the simple definition of Peace is that it is the absence of war, confusion and in Trinidad we'd say no bacchanal! So how can you or anyone recognize a peaceful classroom or school? Well if it's the absence of war, confusion and bacchanal then a peaceful school is one where no gangs exist, no bullies are in control and the activities of young boys and girls are not seen as opportunities for bacchanal. Are we saying that you do not ever have disagreements? No in a real world that is not so but in a peaceful environment, which we at Mac Loughlin High are striving to create, our disagreement will be talked out not bullied out or fought out.

So here is method number 1, to create a peaceful students and stakeholders we must develop an attitude of discussing things through. So to be peaceful, we talk before we fight! We must be pals! Please say that with me *"To be peaceful, we talk before we fight! We must be pals!"* as Form 1s new to this school peace may simply mean speaking softer in class when your teacher is not there and forming a line in the cafeteria.

Peace cannot operate without its partner or pal …Love! *"May true love illumine, as we journey in union"* this line is taken from our school song. So what do you think love is? I know that you have many definitions of what love is. For some love is manifested in the generous and giving actions of their family and friends. For others love is what the God that they serve and believe in shows them by all the blessings that are bestowed on them. Whatever we believe love is, we all know that love is a good human and godly virtue.

Today though I want to join love with peace and tell you that they both depend on each other. That's what pals or friends do! Without peace there is no love and without love there is no peace. So a peaceful class is a loving class and vice versa. You just cannot be fighting, bullying and creating confusion and bacchanal and say that you still love! A peaceful class is a loving class and a loving, peaceful class is a class filled with pals! Again say with me *"A peaceful class is a loving class and a loving and peaceful class is a class filled with pals!"*

In closing, I ask you first formers, *"Do you want your school to be filled with pals and P…A… L…S?"* then I say to every single student in this hall… from today and be it and live it! Be a pal to someone to create PALS in Holy Cross Academy!

Thank you!

This presentation is appropriate as it covered all the areas that I was asked to cover. I presented the first formers who made up the audience with not only an explanation of the theme of peace and love and most of all methods that they can use to demonstrate peace and love in school. The language by way of vocabulary was simple so as the students would understand and the consultative and casual registers both facilitated ease and questions that the students may have.

SECTION C
MODULE 3- SPEAKING AND WRITING

Read the scenario below and answer the questions that follow.

Your Students' Council is on a drive to promote Peace and Love in Schools (PALS). As the President of the Council, you have been asked to address students who have just entered the first form of secondary school, on methods students can employ to demonstrate Peace and Love.

(a) *State the medium/channel you will use to present your message to these students.*
(b) *Compose your message.*
(c) *Write a paragraph explaining/justifying the appropriateness of your presentation.*

Students' response

Good morning everyone, my name is Gerald Graham and I am here to promote Peace and Love in Schools (PALS) and to educate you on how you can employ the methods during your school life at convent. I am most suitable to deliver this message to you all as I am the President of the Student Council here at Dunhill Secondary. Firstly, I will begin by defining and elaborating with the examples of Peace and Love, and then we will discuss what is neither peace nor love in schools and how these methods can be applied to outside situations.

Peace, Peace, Peace… What is Peace? Peace can be defined as an occurrence of harmony characterized by the lack of violence, conflict behaviors and the freedom from fear of violence. Peace can be simply by speaking calmly to your classmates or even resolving conflicts and not holding grudges and looting together as friends try to help each other in the journey of success. *"May true love illumine, as we journey in union"* this line is taken from our school song. So what do you think love is? Love is a virtue representing human kindness, compassion and affection. It is the unselfish loyal good concern for your peers and the compassionate and affectionate actions towards each other and yourself.

Every situation has two sides and so too is this topic of peace and love in schools. We have looked at what is peace and love and now we will be discussing what is not peace and love. Not employing peace and love can lead to arguments, violence, can change school environment to *"fish markets"* and *battlefields* as students would utilize boisterous speaking, hostility and selfishness amongst themselves. This can place a strain on relationships between the lower and upper school students which can promote bullying and can stunt initial growth of students and make the journey to success more difficult. Do you want this?

To employ peace and love at schools, simple gestures can be done such as saying hello, being kind, giving compliments, working in unity to help each other, not discriminating and overall kindness. These methods can also be applied to situations out of school. Being kind to strangers shows respect and can also bring a smile to anyone's face. It can also help you on job sites when you are older. Peace and love is a World Transformation Tool, it begins with one person and can make a difference in the world today.

In conclusion, to recap what we have done, we discussed that peace is the occurrence of harmony characterized by the lack of violence, conflict behaviors and the freedom from fear of violence. We have also said that love is the unselfish loyal good concern for your peers and the compassionate and affectionate actions towards each other and yourself. Finally we have looked at how the methods of peace and love can be used in situations out of school and to generally make the world a better place.

a) The medium and channel I will use to present my message to students are visual aids. A visual aid is an object or representation that can be used to clarify or enhance the understanding of a concept. PowerPoint presentation and short plays are the aids which would be used to show the importance of peace and love in schools. These aids allow both senses of the audience to be utilized i.e. sight and hearing thus aiding in a better understanding of the information. Moreover, they are both ideal choices as young people cannot tolerate too much talking, thus they ensuring their attention is kept throughout.

b) I think my presentation is appropriate as it is simple and to the point. The presentation is not too formal nor too complex in language to create problems with students understanding what is being told, also it is not too long to create a barrier to students such as boredom. It contains methods in which the students can employ peace and love and how it can be applied to situations other than in school. The use of visual aids can also help students remember what is said. The entire presentation is aimed at the form one students so that the skills in peace and love can be instilled in them upon their entry into secondary school.

NB: (a) and (b) are not part of the essay, rather they are responses to specific questions!

SECTION C
MODULE 3- SPEAKING AND WRITING

Read the scenario below and answer the questions that follow.

Your Students' Council is on a drive to promote Peace and Love in Schools (PALS). As the President of the Council, you have been asked to address students who have just entered the first form of secondary school, on methods students can employ to demonstrate Peace and Love.

(a) *State the medium/channel you will use to present your message to these students.*
(b) *Compose your message.*
(c) *Write a paragraph explaining/justifying the appropriateness of your presentation.*

Students' response

a) The medium/channel I will use to present my message to students is either a short PowerPoint or a short skit. PowerPoint presentation and skits as mediums allow both students to engage both their visual and auditory senses. Moreover, they are both ideal choices as young people cannot tolerate too much talking, thus they ensuring their attention is kept throughout.

b) I think my presentation is appropriate as it is simple and to the point. The presentation is not too formal to create problems with students understanding what is being told, also it is not too long to create a barrier to students such as boredom. It contains simple practical methods in which the students can practice peace and love and how it can be applied to situations other than in school. The use of visual aids can also help students remember what is said. The entire presentation is aimed at the form one students so that the skills in peace and love can be instilled in them easily and also reduces the risk of violence in their school thus creating PALS.

Good morning everyone, my name is Belqis Moreno and it's an honour to be back at my alma mater. I am here to promote PALS which is the acronym for Peace and Love in Schools. During my 15 minute presentation I will give you information that is going to show you methods that you as First Formers can use during your school life here at Mac Loughlin High.

First, I will begin by defining and elaborating with the examples of Peace and Love, Secondly, I will discuss what practical methods pertaining to Peace and Love you as students can use to demonstrate PALS.

Peace, Peace, Peace... What is Peace? The dictionary defines Peace as a situation of harmony characterized by the lack of violence, conflict behaviors and the freedom from fear of violence. Some ways that you can spread Peace can be you simply speaking calmly to your classmates or even resolving conflicts, not holding grudges and definitely not being bullies. Yes a bully, a confusion maker, and a loud mouth are not peaceful pals. We want to create pals for PALS in Mac Loughlin!

"May true love illumine, as we journey in union" this line is taken from our school song. So what do you think love is? Love is a virtue manifested in acts of kindness, compassion and affection. It is the unselfish, loyal, good concern that you have for your peers and the compassionate and affectionate actions towards each other and yourself. So when you see a fellow student being shunned or when you realize that a classmate is in need show some love be a pal and you in your own way will be making Mac Loughlin a PALS school!

In closing, the message I leave with you First Formers of MY alma mater is that Peace together with its pal, love is a World Transformation Tool, it begins with one person YOU and ONLY YOU can make a difference in your school today. Go be pals for PALS!

SECTION C
MODULE 3- SPEAKING AND WRITING

Read the scenario below and answer the questions that follow.

Your Students' Council is on a drive to promote Peace and Love in Schools (PALS). As the President of the Council, you have been asked to address students who have just entered the first form of secondary school, on methods students can employ to demonstrate Peace and Love.

(a) *State the medium/channel you will use to present your message to these students.*
(b) *Compose your message.*
(c) *Write a paragraph explaining/justifying the appropriateness of your presentation.*

Students' response

a) The medium/channel I will use to present my message to students is either a short PowerPoint or a short skit. PowerPoint presentation and skits as mediums allow both students to engage both their visual and auditory senses. Moreover, they are both ideal choices as young people cannot tolerate too much talking, thus they ensuring their attention is kept throughout.

b) I think my presentation is appropriate as it is simple and to the point. The presentation is not too formal to create problems with students understanding what is being told, also it is not too long to create a barrier to students such as boredom. It contains simple practical methods in which the students can practice peace and love and how it can be applied to situations other than in school. The use of visual aids can also help students remember what is said. The entire presentation is aimed at the form one students so that the skills in peace and love can be instilled in them easily and also reduces the risk of violence in their school thus creating PALS.

Good morning everyone, my name is Adrian Alexander and it's an honor to be back at my alma mater to address the students of Form 1. I am here to promote PALS, the acronym for Peace and Love in Schools. During my 15 minute presentation I will give you information about some of the methods that you the first form students can use to promote and practice peace and love not only in the school but also outside as well.

Firstly, I will begin by defining and giving examples of the terms Peace and Love.

What is Peace? How do we recognize a peaceful person and situation? Well for many of us the simple definition of Peace is that it is the absence of war, confusion and in Trinidad we'd say no bacchanal! So how can you or anyone recognize a peaceful classroom or school? Well if it's the absence of war, confusion and bacchanal then a peaceful school is one where no gangs exist, no bullies are in control and the activities of young boys and girls are not seen as opportunities for bacchanal. Are we saying that you do not ever have disagreements? No in a real world that is not so but in a peaceful environment, which we at Holy Cross Academy are striving to create, our disagreement will be talked out not bullied out or fought out.

So here is method number 1, to create a peaceful students and stakeholders we must develop an attitude of discussing things through. So to be peaceful, we talk before we fight! We must be pals! Please say that with me "To be peaceful, we talk before we fight! We must be pals!" as Form 1s new to this school peace may simply mean speaking softer in class when your teacher is not there and forming a line in the cafeteria.

Peace cannot operate without …Love! *"May true love illumine, as we journey in union"* this line is taken from our school song. So what do you think love is? I know that you have many definitions of what love is. For some love is manifested in the generous and giving actions of their family and friends. For others love is what the God that they serve and believe in shows them by all the blessings that are bestowed on them. Whatever we believe love is, we all know that love is a good human and godly virtue.

Today though, I want to join love with peace and tell you that they both depend on each other. That's what pals or friends do! Without peace there is no love and without love there is no peace. So a peaceful class is a loving class and vice versa. You just cannot be fighting, bullying and creating confusion and bacchanal and say that you still love! A peaceful class is a loving class and a loving, peaceful class is a class filled with pals! Again say with me "A peaceful class is a loving class and a loving and peaceful class is a class filled with pals!"

In closing, I ask you first formers, "Do you want your school to be filled with pals and P…A… L…S?" then I say to every single student in this hall… from today … be it and live it! Be a pal to someone to create PALS in Holy Cross Academy!

Thank you!

SECTION C
MODULE 3- SPEAKING AND WRITING

Read the scenario below and answer the questions that follow.

You are investigating the effects of cellular telephone use on the population. You decide to do an 'awareness seminar' about the dangers posed by the frequent use of these devices. The seminar will be delivered to a high school population.

a) *In no more than 50 words, explain how you would use TWO visual aids, to enhance your delivery.*

b) *In no more than 300 words, write the feature address, to be delivered at the seminar.*

c) *In your address, discuss at least THREE effects of cellular telephone use on the population.*

Students' response

I would use picture slides in a PowerPoint presentation to illustrate how people are negatively affected by using their cell phones excessively, especially whist driving. A short video presentation would also be used to give a more realistic perspective of the dangers caused by persons who constantly use their cell phones.

Good day to the Principal, vice principal, deans, teachers and students of Crandon High School. Thank you for the invitation to address your school body on the negative effects of the frequent use of the cellular phone or cell as it's commonly called. Although cell phones are necessary for everyday communication in these modern times, they must however, be used in moderation as excessive use can be hazardous in many situations. Now, I know that many of you are thinking I do not drive so this information is not for me but you are sometimes passengers in cars driven by drivers who indulge in behaviours on their cell phones that put human lives at risk.

Firstly, the use of cell phones while driving is highly dangerous to everyone involved. For example as a driver all of your concentration is required to avoid accidents. Making calls and texting or sending a WhatApp messages are all very distracting and in many cases result in serious and or fatal accidents. In order to avoid this I encourage you to desist from using your cell phone while driving. Do not be another statistic! Be smart! If you must take or make a call please pull aside and do so or better yet buy a hands free phone! Don't become a victim!

Another way in which the excessive use of cell phones can endanger your life of the life of others is the possibility of you being the target of robbery with violence. As a student you may have the dangerous habit of using your phone while you are walking on the street. Even though you have been warned you like many others believe that it cannot happen to you, but I am here to tell you that you are so wrong. Do you know that for last year alone 35 students were attacked and their phones stolen and in one instance a student who unwittingly try to resist was stabbed luckily she did not die. Be smart! If you must take or make a call please stop walking, be conscious of your environment t! Do not become a victim!

Lastly, the excessive use of cellular phones can become a distraction if you allow yourself to fall prey to pornography. Some students at this age are curious and that is expected but when you allow yourself to become addicted to pornography that is where it becomes problematic. Cell phones that are in the smartphone or android category can be such a positive addition to the technology that you as a student utilize on a daily basis but like everything else it is not the technology that is bad but the things that you do with the technology. What if when in your desire to quench your pornographic thirst you open up to a pervert? What if this pervert is technology savvy and gets to know your whereabouts? What if he or she begins to stalk you? What are you going to do then? This student is the dangers of the excessive use of cell phones. Be smart! Use your cell phone for things that will help you not bring you down! Do not become a victim!

Thank you for listening and have a blessed day!

SECTION C
MODULE 3- SPEAKING AND WRITING

Read the scenario below and answer the questions that follow.

You are investigating the effects of cellular telephone use on the population. You decide to do an 'awareness seminar' about the dangers posed by the frequent use of these devices. The seminar will be delivered to a high school population.

a) *In no more than 50 words, explain how you would use TWO visual aids, to enhance your delivery.*

b) *In no more than 300 words, write the feature address, to be delivered at the seminar.*

c) *In your address, discuss at least THREE effects of cellular telephone use on the population.*

Students' response

Firstly, I would use an Overhead Transparency showing statistics of road fatalities linked to cell phone use, pictures illustrating the brutal images of road carnage and a video presentation aimed at documenting the negative health and addictive effects associated with excessive use. This enables high visibility in large groups but also the images can have long lasting impacts on the audience.

Good afternoon, students of Sunville High, I am Jerome Beharry, a past student of the college and my purpose this morning is to highlight some of the harmful consequences which the inappropriate and excessive use of cell phones can pose on individuals. With the ever growing omnipresence and rise in popularity of this gadget, it is even more important to take note of the dangers and how they can affect your lives.

One such example which is glaringly obvious is the number of road accidents and deaths. We all notice how the newspapers are littered with endless stories of road tragedy, a fair share which can be attributed to cell phone use. In spite of several studies confirming the inevitable cell phone distraction and concentration deficit behind the wheel increasing the risk significantly of causing road accidents, cell phone use is still quite prevalent in the act of driving. Well I am here to remind you that life is a precious gift and perhaps sometimes taken for granted. We must steer clear of actions detrimental to our lives as well as others. After all, do we want to become a statistic?

Another common problem is that of potential addiction and in particular the susceptibility of youth to fall into this problem. The consequences of being confronted by this worrying situation are quite extensive and range from abysmal academic performance, unwanted economic burden from excessive use, unwillingness to socialize and integrate into wider society, lack of physical activity to feelings of distress when separated from the gadget. Again, I must stress the value of regulating cell phone use or you could be a victim of the ferocious effects above.

Lastly, we must not omit the greater scope of ill effects threatening individual health. According to a study by Swedish researchers, they have established a link between cell phone use and the onset of Alzheimer's disease, leukaemia, brain and mouth cancer and cell phone radiation exposure has been said to be damaging as well. While most of these claims may not be confirmed beyond doubt, it is still imperative to take precautionary measures by way of monitoring our use. If indeed these assertions are true, it would spell disaster in the form of these pernicious health effects. In conclusion, this isn't an anti –cell phone campaign; the cell phone possesses widespread benefits but inconvenient as well and remember we must stay true to the saying *'Prevention is better than cure'*. Think about your well being! The choice is yours.

SECTION C
MODULE 3- SPEAKING AND WRITING

Read the scenario below and answer the questions that follow.

There has been continuous flooding in your community as a result of the habit of extensive littering and deforestation. A group of Sixth Formers from the neighbourhood has decided to launch an awareness campaign to make people accept their responsibility to protect the environment. As a member you have accepted to head the group and to ensure that the campaign is effectively planned and executed.

In an ESSAY of no more than 500 words, discuss how the group proposes to make the campaign effective. Your proposal must address the following areas:

(a) *Maintenance of the theme of the campaign.*
(b) *Targeting of the various audiences involved in the campaign.*
(c) *Use of language(s) in campaign messages.*
(d) *An evaluation of the campaign.*

Students' response

As head of a group responsible for making people aware of their duty to protect the environment, I have been given the task of proposing ways of maintaining the theme of the campaign, target audiences and language used throughout the campaign's messages, and the evaluation of the campaign.

With respect to the theme of the campaign, which is, making people aware of their duty to protect the environment, our group has organized weekly community meetings and a monthly newsletter, all centred on various ways in which an average citizen can help improve the well-being of our environment. Both the meetings and the newsletter would seek to reinforce our theme throughout the community, by offering a gentle reminder of the importance of our environment and suggesting creative and simple methods of existing in synergy with our surrounding environment. Furthermore, we intend to create pages on major social networking sites such as Facebook and Twitter, in an attempt to reach our vast technological generation, that is, community members who are up to date with modern technology and who would find it tedious to attend a weekly meeting.

Moreover, with regards to our target audience, we as a group have found it appropriate to include in our campaign, children between the ages of 5 to 12, teens ages 13 to 19 and young adults 20 to 35. These target audiences were chosen, since they are the future of the community and may soon be in charge of activities and projects taking place within the community, such as the construction of buildings, which may require an act of deforestation which was one of the major factors leading to flooding. We believe that by educating them on the importance of our natural ecosystems, they will be able to find creative, non-destructive ways to blend our community development, with our surrounding environment.

Continuing, we intend to use Creole and Standard English throughout our campaign's messages. The Creole language would be utilized mainly as a means of developing a friendly, comfortable relationship with our target audience, and to make attractive to those who are encouraged to protect the environment. Also, Standard English would be utilized when stating different pieces of information and messages whose content is deemed sensitive and critical in portraying our theme of making people aware of their duty to protect the environment.

Lastly, as a means of evaluating the success of our campaign, we have decided monitor flood reports via our Facebook page where members can responds to short surveys. Suggestion boxes will be placed in strategic positions where members can tell the group what is on their mind when it comes to the topic of flooding and deforestation. We intend to take their responses and suggestions seriously as these are means by which the group can continue its mandate of creating effective public awareness about the issue.

Read the scenario below and answer the questions that follow.

There has been continuous flooding in your community as a result of the habit of extensive littering and deforestation. A group of Sixth Formers from the neighbourhood has decided to launch an awareness campaign to make people accept their responsibility to protect the environment. As a member you have accepted to head the group and to ensure that the campaign is effectively planned and executed.

In an ESSAY of no more than 500 words, discuss how the group proposes to make the campaign effective. Your proposal must address the following areas:

(a) *Maintenance of the theme of the campaign.*
(b) *Targeting of the various audiences involved in the campaign.*
(c) *Use of language(s) in campaign messages.*
(d) *An evaluation of the campaign.*

Students' response

I have been selected to lead the group that will put forward a proposal how to plan and execute the campaign against littering and deforestation in Bel Vue community that have resulted in recent flooding in the area. The group's main objective is to create awareness among the members of the community.

To properly maintain the anti-littering and deforestation themes of the campaign the group would print and put up bright red and green posters throughout the community which would depict scenes of the recent floods and the destruction that they left in the aftermath. This strategy would not only create awareness but it would put a degree of fear in the members that would result in most if not all of them accepting their responsibility to protect their environment.

A Website and a matching Facebook page titled *"Go Green Bel Vue"* would be established where the group would post pertinent information about the topic such as simple methods of prevention and the causes of flooding and deforestation. The website and Facebook page would also have photo galleries of *'before'* and *'after'* pictures as well as a section where individuals will make a pledge to be more environmentally friendly and what activity that they have done to do so. This strategy of using mass media and the social network is ideal for targeting various audiences according to age, gender, preference and profession.

In order to reach our mature adults and the elderly in our audience, thirty second advertisements placed right before the prime time nightly news report on the television and radio would catch their attention. On the television the advertisement would feature a montage of photos of the recent flood against a background of melancholy music. The narrating voice will tell the viewer that Bel Vue must never again fall prey to the ravages of deforestation that resulted in the damaging effects of floods. The radio however, would only have the narration and the music. This strategy capitalises on the fact that the majority of older members always listen or tune in to the nightly news and they will see or hear the advertisement.

An assortment of T-shirts and buttons with anti-littering and deforestation logos will be distributed along with pamphlets which would contain methods to reduce littering and deforestation would be handed throughout the community effectively branding and marketing the campaign as most individual would be eager to collect 'free' items.

The language employed would be Standard English and the register formal to reach the adults in the community and to emphasise the severity of the situation. On the other hand, to reach the younger members of the community who in most cases tend to appreciate a more casual approach by way of the Creole language which in all instances gives a sense nationalistic pride as we try to reach the community.

The success of our campaign as with any other relies heavily on the evaluation strategies that we employ and for this reason we intend to conduct surveys to solicit feedback responses from the community. On our website and Facebook page we also intend to use them as agents of evaluation. At public and private businesses and institutions we would place suggestion boxes so yet again the members of the community would have an avenue to voice concerns and suggestion on the issue. Evaluation via feedback would be continuous for at least a six month period if the campaign is to be effective.

SECTION C
MODULE 3- SPEAKING AND WRITING

Read the scenario below and answer the questions that follow.

There has been continuous flooding in your community as a result of the habit of extensive littering and deforestation. A group of Sixth Formers from the neighbourhood has decided to launch an awareness campaign to make people accept their responsibility to protect the environment. As a member you have accepted to head the group and to ensure that the campaign is effectively planned and executed.

In an ESSAY of no more than 500 words, discuss how the group proposes to make the campaign effective. Your proposal must address the following areas:

(a) *Maintenance of the theme of the campaign.*
(b) *Targeting of the various audiences involved in the campaign.*
(c) *Use of language(s) in campaign messages.*
(d) *An evaluation of the campaign.*

Students' response

As a member of the environmental awareness group in my neighbourhood, I have been assigned to head the group and to ensure the campaign is effectively planned and executed. The aim of this campaign is to promote environmental awareness. The target audience will comprise of the general public inclusive of the working class, the students, stay home persons, professionals and self employed.

Since I'm the head of the group, it is my duty to ensure the theme of protecting our neighbourhood from the ravages of floods is maintained in order for the message to be received and understood. This theme will be maintained by the use of a variety of medium/channels. Firstly I would consider the use of various verbal presentations in the form of calypsos, dramatic presentations, lecture discussions, documentaries, electronic billboard advertisements and flyers quite appropriate in promoting and maintaining the theme of environmental protection. I chose these various verbal presentations because both young persons and adults enjoy listening to topics that are their focus and also persons generally tend to remember the message of dramatic verbal presentations.

Additionally, I have catered for those in my audience who are more visually inclined by way of electronic billboard advertisements and flyers which will visually impact the audience thus allowing them to both understand and remember the message of the campaign.

The channels which I would use include internet, hand held digital technology, television, radio, billboards and the newspapers. The fact that these channels are popular among the different age groups are unquestionable, there will be a higher possibility that the message will be received. Finally, the campaign would span for nine months to ensure that the message will be well received. The use of media and channel will ensure effective maintenance of the theme.

As the target audience involves the general public, a variety of strategies will be put forth to educate the different age groups. Firstly, primary school students, there will be quizzes and essay writing competitions. These will allow more self-learning on the topic. Additionally, there can be debating competitions and dramatic presentations like talk tents which can be held in secondary schools. Both these activities will also promote self-learning of the topic. In both primary and secondary schools, the strategies will be successful as students tend to challenge themselves by going up for competitions, as well as to gain certificates of participation for university. For the older persons, there can be conventions and open forums throughout the different communities. These conventions and forums will be free; environmental protection will be discussed and these adults will be able to ask questions on the topic. These strategies will allow for the message to be truly understood and accepted.

The use of language will determine both the connectivity with the audience and the acceptability of a message. Given the gravity of the topic and the urgency in ensuring that the message is sent to the various audiences the language used will be both Standard English and our Creole vernacular. The vocabulary chose will be simple with minimal technical or complex words or phrases. The tone as far as possible will be conversational and narrative.

Finally, to determine the success of the campaign, it must be evaluated. Various research methods will be employed such as observations, to note whether or not the litter practices are upheld or discontinued; questionnaires will be handed out to or sent out in digital or hard copy to sample groups both at the beginning and the conclusion of the campaign so as to gain feedback on whether they are going to change their lifestyle to become more environmentally friendly or whether they have not. A face book page or a website will also keep the group up to date because they both allow persons to give comments.

SECTION C
MODULE 3- SPEAKING AND WRITING

Read the scenario below and answer the questions that follow.

There has been continuous flooding in your community as a result of the habit of extensive littering and deforestation. A group of Sixth Formers from the neighbourhood has decided to launch an awareness campaign to make people accept their responsibility to protect the environment. As a member you have accepted to head the group and to ensure that the campaign is effectively planned and executed.

In an ESSAY of no more than 500 words, discuss how the group proposes to make the campaign effective. Your proposal must address the following areas:

(a) *Maintenance of the theme of the campaign.*
(b) *Targeting of the various audiences involved in the campaign.*
(c) *Use of language(s) in campaign messages.*
(d) *An evaluation of the campaign.*

Students' response

As head of a group responsible for making people aware of their duty to protect the environment, I have been given the task of maintaining the theme of the campaign, suggesting target audiences and language used throughout the campaign's messages, and the evaluation of the campaign.

With respect to the theme of the campaign, that is, making people aware of their duty to protect the environment, our group has organized weekly community meetings and a monthly newsletter, all centred and focused on various ways in which an average citizen can help improve the well-being of our environment. Both the meetings and the newsletter would seek to reinforce our theme throughout the community, by offering a gentle reminder of the importance of our environment and suggesting creative and simple methods of existing in synergy with our surrounding environment. Furthermore, we intend to create pages on major social networking sites such as Facebook and Twitter, in an attempt to reach our vast technological generation, that is, community members who are up to date with modern technology and who would find it tedious to attend a weekly meeting.

Moreover, with regards to our target audience, we as a group have found it appropriate to include in our campaign, children between the ages of 5 to 12, teens ages 13 to 19 and young adults 20 to 35. These target audiences were chosen, since they are the future of the community and may soon be in charge of activities and projects taking place within the community, such as the construction of buildings, which may require an act of deforestation which was one of the major factors leading to flooding. We believe that by educating them on the importance of our natural ecosystems, they will be able to find creative, non-destructive ways to blend our community development, with our surrounding environment.

Continuingly, we intend to use Creole and Standard English throughout our campaign's messages. The Creole language would be occupied mainly as a means of developing a friendly, comfortable relationship with our target audience, and to make attractive to those who are encouraged to protect the environment. Also, Standard English would be utilized when stating different pieces of information and messages whose content is deemed sensitive and critical in portraying our theme of making people aware of their duty to protect the environment.

Lastly, as a means of evaluating the success of our campaign, we have decided monitor flood reports within the community to measure if there was a decrease or an increase of floods. Also, we would keep a close eye on reported cases of deforestation and littering to see whether there were increases or decreases in such reports.

SECTION C
MODULE 3 - SPEAKINGAND WRITING

Read the following scenario carefully and then answer the question that follows.

Your community has decided to host a Family Day. You have been selected to serve as Public Relations Officer. You have been given substantial funds to promote the Family Day and you have been mandated to target the adolescents in the community. In an ESSAY of no more than 500 words, discuss the plan of action that you propose to undertake to promote the Family Day. Your plan must include the following:

    (a) Three strategies for reaching the adolescents in the community, and one way of achieving each strategy

    (b) Language registers and varieties that would be considered appropriate

    (c) How your knowledge of the process of communication would help you to conduct a successful promotion.

Total 25 marks

Students' response

For our upcoming community Family Day, there is a concern with getting the adolescents of our community to attend the event. I have been asked to serve in the capacity of Public Relations Officer of the Family Day therefore it is my duty to use strong and effective strategies in my campaign to influence young adult members of the community to attend this event. I will now propose three strategies that will achieve this along with the language registers and varieties that I consider appropriate.

Teens today are constantly connected to the internet therefore the first strategy would be to use technology to get the information out to them. One way to do this is the creation of a Facebook page. This page would be able to reach a large number of teenagers who frequent this social networking site. The page would be colourful, interesting and give the details of the family day. A mixture of Creole and Standard English would be used for informality in order to appeal to the fun and lighter side of the event. This would make the event appealing to teens who would not want to attend if they think it would be boring and formal as well as to make the page more likely to be shared with other teenagers.

Additionally, radio and television advertisements incorporating the latest soca songs and catchy jingles would be made and placed on the stations popular with teens. These include Star947, Boom Champions and TV6. The ads would be written in a mixture of Creole and

Standard English which, along with the jingles and songs, would add memorability and grab the attention of the teenagers.

Finally, the last strategy would be to give out flyers and place banners throughout the community, especially in the well trafficked areas like recreation areas, shops and taxi stands. These flyers and banners would be colourful, easy to read and highlight the activities that young people would mostly be interested in, for example the DJ and guest artiste that will be present on the day. The information will be given in Standard English and in a simple and concise manner. These flyers and banners will be seen by both young and old and the adolescents would be drawn to the Family Day if they know that there will be a popular DJ and that there are events that they will be willing to participate in.

In order to conduct a successful promotion, knowledge of the communication process is essential. This knowledge would help as I would be able to get my message across to my target audience clearly and get the desired feedback. I would be able to correctly choose the most appropriate media to reach adolescents and this also would give me the ability to properly create my message so that it gives the relevant information and persuades the receiver to attend our Family Day.

The strategies proposed, if put in place; will be effective in resulting in a successful Family Day. They are appropriate and will reach the teenagers and all other member of our community.

SECTION C
MODULE 3- SPEAKING AND WRITING

Read the scenario below and answer the questions that follow.

You are a member of the Abstinence Club in your high schools. You are concerned about the small number of students that attend your weekly meetings. You have been asked to organise a campaign that would convince students to attend meetings.

In an ESSAY of no more than 500 words, write a proposal for your advertising campaign. Include the following:

(a) *Strategies you would use to attract students to the club meetings and justification for these strategies*

(b) *Language varieties and registers you would consider appropriate*

(c) *The information you think must be relayed during this campaign.*

Total 25 marks

Students' response

The poor attendance to our Abstinence Club meetings at school is a matter of grave concern. Thus, I have been asked to organize a campaign to convince students to attend meetings. For the success of the campaign strategies to attract students, language varieties, registers and the information to be included in this campaign must be carefully addressed.

The most important factor to consider when selecting campaign strategies is the audience and its demographics such as religious beliefs, age and gender. I propose that at every Monday morning whole school assembly a standing advertisement which would remind and encourage members and potential members will be presented. This advertisement will vary in formats such as a dance, short play, spoken word poetry, traditional poem, and letter to the editor, monologue or dialogue. These will be chosen because they are able to utilize be the verbal and non-verbal forms of communication thus ensuring that we keep the interest level high which in turn will lead to regular attendance to the meeting.

Posters and social media such as Facebook and Twitter will be utilized to reach our audience of students even when they are not in school. On a Facebook page set up specifically for the promotion of the school's Abstinence Club will broadcast time of meetings, events, visits of personalities and relevant information. Members will be identified by the T-shirts that will carry the club's monogram and motto and also members who stay on for a year with the club will be recognised by the badge that they will be given for their service and regular attendance.

Language used to communicate both in the meeting and in the information about the club will be both of the Standard and the Creole variety. Standard will be utilized in instances like the advertisements and on the Facebook page and Twitter account because both these mediums are mass media with a potentially wide local, regional and international audience. The Creole variety will be used when talking and interacting with the students about not too serious matters and as such the informal register is created. Likewise when Standard English is used both the formal and the consultative registers are created. In the consultative register there will be opportunities for the members to ask their questions and receive answers to them thus boosting the attendance.

Finally, but certainly not the least important, I will address the information which will be relayed during the campaign. I propose that meeting days and time be made known regularly throughout the campaign so as to remind students to attend. Making the benefits known up front is all the influence that some students need to attend so I propose that some of the benefits of attending the Abstinence club be relayed during the campaign. Past events could also be featured so as to encourage potential students to attend.

In conclusion, addressing the strategies to be used to attract potential students, the language varieties and registers to be used in the campaign and the information that must be relayed will ensure the success of the campaign.

SECTION C
MODULE 3- SPEAKING AND WRITING

Read the scenario below and answer the questions that follow.

The prefect body at your school has decided to organize a campaign promoting a healthy lifestyle among the school community. As a student of the Communication Studies class, you have been asked to develop a proposal for presentation to the principal.

In an essay of no more that 500 words, present

(i)   Your proposal, including such items as theme, timetable of events, personnel to be involved and benefits to the school

(ii) Justification for at least THREE specific strategies to be used to promote the campaign.

Total 25 marks

Student's response

In today's environment of fast pace and much distractions, persons battle with many health issues which invariably comes down to this question, "To be healthy or not to be healthy?" The prefect body of my school has recognised this issue and has decided that the entire school community should embark on what we call "The New You is the Healthy You" campaign. As the one with the responsibility of developing the proposal that will be presented to the principal we have decided on a holistic approach to this healthy lifestyle. A month long campaign is our plan if there is to have any life time or life changing effect on the population of our school community which include the students of upper and lower school, the male and female teachers, the administrators, the auxiliary staff and the interested parents..

Our theme "The New You is the Healthy You" promotes the idea that any individual (young or old) must make a conscious choice to be healthy because short of sounding cliché we in the Communication Studies class believe that a person's health is his or her insurance to wealth. The premier event to begin this month of events geared towards the school community making healthy lifestyle choices is the lecture seminar conducted by three of our past pupils who agreed to spend that day with their alma mater. Attendees will be grouped in terms of age, so in essence we are having 3 lectures seminars happening concurrently at different locations around the school. Each lecture will be half hour long (taking into consideration attention span) and thus following will be half hour question and answer session. A break where participants may mix and mingle will be given at this point. After the break there will be an hour group session where the participants will devote the time to putting their creative skills together to put together a 10 minute presentation when the three groups come together at the end of the day. Each group must present on the topic of the morning lecture.

The second event scheduled will be a Food Fair where again the school community will be privy to practical ways to embrace the healthy lifestyle that will create the "New you". Parents will be invited to set up booths where all foods will be given as samples. Foods made from organic stuff will also be for sample. Healthy fruit and vegetable smoothies, raw foods, salads from vegetables and fruits, local fruit chows and much more will be available. This day will end with a Zumba Work out with our resident Zumba teacher, Miss Kathy.

The third event will be a Walkathon through the community. Getting permission from the relevant authorities such as the Police and getting an ambulance on stand –by is easy as we have asked the parents who work in these places to do that part of the preparation for us. Because it is a school day the students will be asked to wear their physical education House uniform. This Walkathon will also allow this idea of "The New You is the Healthy You "to be spread to the wider community.

Concomitantly with the events are the strategies that would eventually lead to the success of this month long healthy lifestyle campaign. Firstly we propose to use make and use fliers to appeal to the section of the school community who would seek logic and reason as to why it's imperative that they make healthy life choices. On theses fliers we will put enough but not too much statistics from credible sources in the field of healthy eating and lifestyle choices. The fliers will also be used to give the dates and times of events of the campaign.

For the tech-savvy population of the school we propose to reach them via our website and Facebook event page. Again the pertinent information such as dates and times and topics and special events pertaining to the theme of the month campaign will be posted. The Facebook page and website will also be used to collect suggestions on how to better this campaign if it were to be held as an annual event.

The school environment will not be left out; we propose to put up a large banner to the front of the school encouraging all to participate. In each classroom we will have artistic students create posters about the event or about specific event. Throughout the month so as to ensure that interest is kept at the maximum, prizes via daily competitions will be given away.

We know that this can be a success if each group within the school community such as the students, teachers, auxiliary staff, administration and interested stakeholders are specifically targeted. "The New You is the Healthy You" is a great way of ensuring that persons make informed choices about their lifestyle.

48.   TRIBUTE TO MY STUDENTS

As a teacher, over the years I have realised a good compliment I can give to my students is to tell them that their essay is of such a standard worthy to be kept in my file to be used as Sample Essays in future classes. Today in this text I seek to pay them the highest compliment of 'immortalizing' their work.

My tribute goes out to the students of:

Bishop Anstey High School Port of Spain
class of 2010 and 2011

Students of St. Mary's College
2010, 2011, 2012

Holy Faith Convent, Couva
2012, 2013 and 2014

About the Author

EDLIN D. ROCHFORD'S teaching career spans pre-school to tertiary education. She holds a double major in History and Literatures in English, Diploma in Education and a Masters in Reading from The University of The West Indies. Edlin is an Examiner for Communication Studies at the annual marking exercise in Jamaica. She is married to Philip and resides in Couva Trinidad.

AUTHOR'S CONTACT INFORMATION

Edlin Dianne Rochford
e-mail: edlinrochford@gmail.com